Mission. Staying on course. Knowing the answer to Why? before committing to How? Pragmatism can rip the soul out of mission. Deborah Benson takes to task the calcified conditions of human-centered educational philosophies and models, while leaving the reader with a thoroughly biblical approach to Christian education. "The stranger" has been the responsibility of God's people since the beginning (Leviticus 19:33–34) and will become our neighbor when we practice the mission principles of *Graciously Unapologetic.* Benson's book should break the stultifying, stagnating, strangulating perspectives and practices resident within Christian schooling. Benson's book gives proof that ancient truths are perennial ideals. Her incessant questioning should bring about a mission renewal for every Christian school.

Mark Eckel, **Ph.D., President**
The Comenius Institute, Indianapolis, Indiana

Deborah Benson has been immersed in Christian education for more than 45 years. From her days at the feet of her pastor-father to her time as a student to enrolling and supporting her own children to teaching and now leading in Christian schools, Ms. Benson has been a lifelong advocate for distinctively Christ-centered education. It has been one of my deepest privileges to witness her growth as she battled her own inconsistencies to live out of love rather than fear. *Graciously Unapologetic* is less a culmination of experiences and more a waypoint on her journey toward a deeper understanding of how to teach Christ and build school cultures and programs that are beautifully anchored in God's grace in Christ alone.

Chad Dirkse, **President**
Chattanooga Christian School, Chattanooga, Tennessee

We are called, and even commanded, to live with, love, and serve all those with whom we come into contact, both those near to Christ and those far off. How dare we, as Christian schools, avoid or even outright refuse to reflect Christ in all ways, to all people? In *Graciously Unapologetic* Deborah Benson explains how fear rather than love has driven much of the "doing" in Christian school communities. She reminds us through carefully selected scriptural references that Who are we to be? is a more pressing question than What shall we do? This book is both convicting and motivating, as the author offers experiential insight into the current degrading spiritual state of Christian schools and provides direction for moving Christian educators and administrators further in obedience to reflecting Christ's glory through a balance of Grace and Truth.

Robin Oudyn, math teacher and Christian school parent
Parkview Christian Academy, Yorkville, Illinois

Christian schools today are filed with fear—fear of going out of business, fear of the culture around them, fear of those who are not Christian. Deborah Benson makes a heartfelt and scholarly plea to think about teaching in the light of God's call to love, to cast out fear, and to care for the sojourner/foreigner/unbeliever in the land. This call to excellence from God's point of view is sorely needed in a society where Christian witness has lost its salt. An interesting and compelling educational argument with deeply spiritual underpinnings!

Simon Jeynes, Director
Christian School Management, Wilmington, Delaware

Benson issues a clarion call to Christian schools to live up to their missions, using the lens of student admissions to rethink what it means to both stick to biblical principles and be the witness to our neighbors Christ asks us to be. Christian school boards, administrators, and teachers would do well to read, discuss, and act upon this timely and thought-provoking book!

Dan Beerens, independent consultant and CACE Fellow

I was both inspired and convicted by this book—without a guilt trip, though. Deb Benson lives what she has written in this seminal piece of writing. She herself is a sojourner in a life dedicated to Christlikeness and authentic

Christian education. Ideas in the book gave me excellent new insights into dealing with the "seeker" and "discipling" in the context of Christian schools. Revival of Christian schools in an age of moral relativism and blasé parental responses to education could result from serious consideration of the ideas in Deb's book. Such revival is possible only in humility and with an honesty that would allow for the proper mix of grace and truth of which Deb writes in her book. I was an English teacher and I am an avid writer, but I have seldom discovered a writer with a greater grasp of vocabulary in stating profound ideas; Deb's intellect and writing ability have allowed her to carefully craft sentences in a tome that will need to be read over and over again by Christian educators and boards that are dedicated to seeing Christian schools thrive and not just survive. Our educational era so desperately needs the redemption of people, as well as the redemption of learning that can come only through Jesus Christ and the direction of the Holy Spirit. Deb's book is rock-solid theologically and philosophically sound. READ . . . THIS . . . BOOK!

Bob Stouffer, Ph.D., Principal
Oskaloosa Christian School, Oskaloosa, Iowa

If you are reading this book in your role as a Christian educator, head of school, or board member, I can promise you one thing. At some point, you will put this book down, perhaps even angrily. You will go off and think about what you've read, and then return to continue the journey. Whether you are covenantal or missional in your purpose, this book is a clarion call bringing us back to the Word of God as the source of why we do what we do. It calls us to examine whether Christ is reflected in our *Christian* schools. Read on, I dare you!

Joel Westra, President/CEO
Christian Schools International, Grand Rapids, Michigan

One way to make sense of our current educational landscape is to look at how and where we have strayed from a Christ-centered existence. *Graciously Unapologetic* teaches us much about those concepts, but more than that, we are given a tool to help us stay faithful to our task as Christian educators and to know what that truly means.

Micah Johnson, **Bible teacher**
Parkview Christian Academy, Yorkville, Illinois

This is an unsettling work, one that nudges at the edges or your heart, that will stretch and challenge you. It calls us into obedient service of a God who is sovereign and faithful—to more deeply love and trust this God and to allow his grace to unravel the fear that binds and limits us. Ultimately, the book is a clarion call for our Christian institutions to be places where God's truth is boldly proclaimed and lavishly accessible.

Randy Moes, **Principal**
Calvin Christian School, Grandville, Michigan

What a privilege and humbling honor it has been to read and absorb the comprehensive and challenging thinking about the true heart of Christian education! In *Graciously Unapologetic*, Deborah Byker-Benson has outlined many significant biblical challenges so that we may offer "Christ alone" as the what, how, and why of true Christian schooling. Insight into the impact of her recommendation on the entire structure of the school from board to student is refreshing, thought provoking, and rich with scriptural applications. A must-read for anyone who is part of the Christian education experience.

Judy Vos, **teacher, administrator, and consultant (retired)**
Pella Christian Schools, Pella, Iowa

GRACIOUSLY UNAPOLOGETIC

Grace + Truth
to you,
Deborah Byker
Benner

GRACIOUSLY UNAPOLOGETIC

A RENEWED WAY TO BE IN CHRISTIAN SCHOOLS

DEBORAH BYKER-BENSON

Graciously Unapologetic

Published in the United States by Credo House Publishers,
a division of Credo Communications, LLC, Grand Rapids, Michigan
www.credohousepublishers.com

ISBN: 978-1-625860-37-8

Cover design by Marc Whitaker
Interior design by PerfecType, Nashville, TN
Editing by Donna Huisjen

Printed in the United States of America

First edition

To my dear friends **Chad** and **Heather Dirkse**.

Your grace and truth toward me is the seed that sprouted, took root, and grew into this book. Without you, there would have been no book.

CONTENTS

1

Why Renewal?

The need to consider a renewed way of being in Christian schools follows a number of long-standing issues. Fear-dominated governance and leadership have made a way for contradictory practice and policy, widespread academic mediocrity, and theological fluctuation. Now concerns about sustainability heighten as reciprocal influences, such as the speed of change, widespread immorality, and affluence, plague the landscape. Increasing polarization and growing numbers of Christian school closings add to the fears. All of these disturbing indicators add lurid color to the institutional landscape.

If these concerns are well placed, a student of the Bible and of history will not be shocked by them. What might be disturbing is the lack of spiritual analysis as a response, of courage to challenge conviction, and of biblical leadership as opposed to religious management. Asking Christian school leaders to set aside discussions about teaching strategies and indicators of learning in order to wrestle with the spiritual principles underlying the organizational landscape evokes a predominant response of patronizing disinterest. The conversations quickly return to "what to do" rather than "who to be." The problem is that one cannot rightly know "what to do" if not first settled on "who to be."

This book seeks to diagnose and suggest treatment for the spiritual illness at the root of all these concerning symptoms. Excellence demands measurement, and Christian schools are responding intensely with this activity. Sadly, many imagine that intense measuring, strategizing, and social media networking around best practice comprise a heroic effort to "do the right thing" while catching up to the culprit, the speed of change. I am a willing participant in the heroic effort, but which spiritual error(s) prohibited "the right things" several decades ago while change was speeding and Christian schools were sufficiently dysfunctional not to notice? Is it safe to assume the "right things" are being done in a right spiritual framework after decades of mediocrity?

Are the heroic efforts driven by a desire to reflect the right way to be or simply by a response to alarming indicators? Is the passion of this decade about teaching Christ or about fear of extinction in a value driven culture? Is it proactive or reactive? Merely reactive strategies will probably measure content learning, but definitely not spiritual health. Reactive strategies to ensure institutional survival are taking solid precedence over a proactive way of being Christ-like.

I contend that the root of the spiritual problem is the fear (reactive) that chokes out the love (proactive). Organizationally, fear results primarily in ways of being controlling. What if "due diligence" is hiding prejudicial processes, or "Christian kids" are resulting from guilt manipulated "goodness," or "world class academics" are euphemistically masking empty intellectualism? Does it matter what lies beneath the wide array of buzzwords adopted to drive heroic efforts? Heroic "right" choices and actions are in overwhelming abundance. But "right" does not erase the wrong of apathy toward spiritual dysfunction.

That Christian schools have suffered from spiritual dysfunction is not new news. Symptomatic recognition is not the problem; a lack of interest in the disease and in a proactive response *is*. The predominantly reactive response to symptoms is arguably advancing the disease, resulting in less "being" and more "doing." Underlying dysfunction will remain and flourish until recognized and replaced by a renewed way of being Christ-like.

For example, one prominent effort underway to address spiritual symptoms is the identification, quantification, and measurement of spiritual or faith formation. One frequently stated objective of the effort is to demonstrate distinction in forming faith and spiritualism, thereby rendering a Christian education worth the financial sacrifice in a value-add culture. These laudable efforts to do something about mediocrity in training on matters of faith take place in a context that has a notable absence of statements that "out" the pride, self-righteousness, and hypocrisy that have led to poor accountability and lack of passion for excellence in the first place. Would it be wise if Christian educators spend time asking what *way of being* in sin had caused this problem? And what alternate *way of being* would renew spiritual strength and cause Christian educators to soar on wings like eagles (Isaiah 40:31)?[1]

To teach is to form knowledge, and to assess is to measure knowledge learned. Efforts to measure faithful inputs to learning in the knowledge of God, both cognitive and affective (head and hands), are obedient (Psalm 78:4),[2] but these efforts in best practice cannot form, guarantee, or assess the presence of faith or spirituality (heart). Spirituality flows from the heart (Proverbs 4:23),[3] while faith is a gift from above (Ephesians 2:8).[4] People and organizations accountable to faithful teaching grow in faith and spirituality. They become reliant upon Christ, while boldly sharing the blessings of His fellowship and vehemently disavowing satisfaction with any kind of mediocrity. Are Christian schools in jeopardy from failure to "do stuff," or did a failure to *be* something integrally reflective of Christ lead to spiritual dysfunction, followed by heads full of contradiction, hands that have grown lazy, and hearts filled with pride?

Could it be that to measure and market Christian education on the basis of faith or spiritual formation are themselves evidences of a dysfunctional way of being. The faith and spiritual formation efforts are rectifying a lack of excellence and accountability in the teaching and learning of the knowledge and integration of Truth, and rightly so. But naming and selling these efforts as "faith or spiritual formation," as opposed to identifying these efforts more aptly as a return to proactive obedience out of love, leads participants to understand spiritual life and faith as a series of acts and choices—as theater. This approach also exposes an alarming erosion in organizational understandings of the relationship between the principles that are professed (faith is a gift) and the practices engaged in the work (faith is formed by the right work).

What is Christian education if not an array of glimpses into spiritual reality, intentionally designed to display the vastness and completeness of Christ in all content and process? Every minute detail of Christian school life is a sin/sanctified mixture of intentional efforts to teach the undiluted truth and to rest in the unlimited grace that must be relentlessly resolved in Christ alone. Where this resolution, this array of glimpses, is proactively pursued in love, fear grows strangely irrelevant. As fear subsides, the need for control lessens and a graciously unapologetic way of being takes root and flourishes.

Who's to blame for this mess? All of us. Several biblical traditions flow into the dysfunction, each ultimately fed by a wellspring of fear about the wrong things. Over time, fear of the wrong things results in weighty omission(s) of the mandates of the law—like the biblical injunction to trust in God (Proverbs 3:5–6; Matthew 23:23–24).[5] The suggestion of this book is intended as a unifying biblical principle as a basis for moving toward spiritual health. Traditions, denominations, and congregations are horribly fragmented and inconsistent, and none of them alone can address the widespread problem. What matters now is that lovers of teaching Christ, of any tradition, find a renewed and unified way of being Christ-like. By all means we should keep on doing heroic things, but we would be spiritually healthy, and God willing, organizationally sound, when we were all doing them on the unchanging spiritual foundation of Christ alone.

I'll confess first. My career in Christian education (and my parenting) began with fear rather than love. I called my attempts at control "love." I was "loving" God by seeking control, helping Him to produce my desired results. I was full of pride, afraid of exposure, and self-protective. I taught Christ *and* my principles, my law, my checked boxes, my comfortable community. My controls made grace easy and truth safe. In my blindness I hid Christ far more than I reflected Him.

But I was forcibly turned toward Christ as my graciously unapologetic exemplar in all of life's content and process. Because Christ is the standard (John 1:14),[6] every day is a success (2 Corinthians 12:9).[7] His righteousness completes what I have left undone (Philippians 3:9),[8] and His sacrifice satisfies the demand of a law I cannot keep (Matthew 22:37–39).[9]

To summarize bluntly, the love of God that drove the establishment of Christian schools on North American soil contained enough fear to motivate controlled environments and/or manipulated manifestations of faith that are now entombed in biblically incomplete school models and spiritually dysfunctional ways of being Christ-like. For the most part schools are arguably stingy with grace and/or apologetic about truth. That the anchor won't hold is an appropriate concern. A renewed way of being spiritual (as opposed to merely traditional or blindly dysfunctional) can only begin with a proactive and loving reflection of the limitless grace and unyielding truth of Jesus Christ in all content and process. That anchor alone will hold. We only have to let it down.

> "If my people, that are called by my name, will humble themselves, and pray, and seek my face, and turn from their wicked ways; then will I hear from heaven, and will forgive their sin, and will heal their land." (2 Chronicles 7:14, KJV)

2

A Renewed Model

It's easy to fall in love with an organizational model. But when faced with ominous indicators one might explore biblical principles in search of a renewed model on which to base a renewed way of being spiritual. Models are helpful tools, but even the best are designed and influenced by fallen people. That a model was designed by some individuals who were admired, and even who had some biblical pattern in mind, does not render it infallible, transcendent, or eternal. Stands to reason a "re-do" might be in order—or at least deserving of careful consideration.

Current Christian school models are predominantly predicated on one or both of two assumptions: that (1) the Christian school community can and should be protected from outside influences, using pre-qualifiers designed by men and women, and that (2) the Christian school community is a place where salvation can be recognized, managed, or manipulated, using a variety of qualifiers designed by human beings. In content, school models derived from any Protestant biblical tradition would *teach* that only God knows the *who*, *when*, and *how* of salvation and kingdom building. In process, however, they often *show* the opposite, both through pre-qualifiers to enrollment and through outward manipulations of faith-like actions *in* others, as opposed to reflecting living faith in Christ *to* others.

Consider whether "teaching Christ in all content and process" is the only appropriate function of a Christ-affiliated school. The establishment of a Christian school is an act of obedience and worship, a loving and proactive response to God's command to *teach Christ*. Reflecting Christ in process (a way to be), while integrating Him in content (what to do), is a loving, obedient, and powerful means God promises to use toward His ends, both in building the kingdom and in saving souls. But loving God and neighbor while teaching Christ requires letting go of fear controls designed to help God with kingdom building and soul winning. It also implies a model that is different from those in popular use today.

Ponder for a few moments the assertions of Acts 2:39: "The promise is to you and to your children" and "to those that are afar off, as many as the Lord will call."

Decades of spiritual dysfunction have resulted in hopes of saving, protecting, controlling, manipulating, measuring, engineering, and isolating faith within the Christian school environment. It is particularly urgent that Christian schools move toward a model that aims at *teaching Christ alone*, at focusing solely on the One in whom all hope for the future lies. God promises Christ both within the line of generations (verse 39a) and also to those "afar off" (39b). Christian schools are predominantly patterned with a bias toward the "a" or the "b" of this pivotal verse, using various forms of control to manage the outward results of the bias and consequently modeling more what is feared than what is loved and trusted. Salvation and its fruit result from the righteousness and sacrifice of Christ alone, as applied by His Word and Spirit. The Christian school is called simply to teach Christ in love first toward God and then toward one's neighbor, without fear (Matthew 22:36-40; 1 John 4:18).[1]

Inherited models of Christian education have been effective formats for schooling because they reflect the primary purpose of God in Christian community: namely, to "feed my sheep" (John 21:15–17)[2] within the line of generations (read also Deuteronomy 6:1–15 and Psalm 78), while renewing and conforming minds toward His likeness. Whether driven by a focus on Acts 2:39a or on 39b, Christian school models have rested on a foundation that includes the support of churches, Christian parents, and Christian school leaders. Embedded in this arrangement is a community predominantly unified by similar ideals, sharing the burden of work and resources (verses 44–47).[3] The church, home, and school arrangement remains an integral platform for effective Christian schooling.

Before continuing, I should note that references in this book to persons in formal affiliation with or in a Christ-affiliated community are not intended to be synonymous references to saved persons. Faith communities are always a mixture (Matthew 13:24–30)[4]; God alone knows the hearts that He will mold and strengthen (1 Samuel 16:7).[5] For purposes of this book, then, a believer is defined as the undeserving recipient (Romans 3:9–11)[6] of Grace (Ephesians 2:8–10)[7] and Truth (John 17:17–19),[8] perfectly and completely balanced upon the righteousness and sacrifice of Christ. There is complete causation between receiving faith and producing fruit, in that order. On the other hand, there is only minimal correlation (and no causation) between outward acts and the presence of faith.

With that in mind, this book offers a renewed model, based on the pattern of Acts 2:39, to under-gird a renewed way of being Christ-like. In spite of many polite conversations about why this or that model should be followed, it may simply be that neither of the predominant choices is complete. If leaders in Christian schools believe they are in crisis, I would challenge them in blunt terms to wrestle toward a firm resting place on a unified biblical pattern that requires teaching Christ alone—not on one or another comfortable tradition. It seems clear that the predominantly reactive ways of exerting control (while being bipolar about Christ) fail to constitute effective, sustainable, or fully biblical foundations on which to teach Christ in these perilous times.

The model pictured below represents proactive obedience to the commands of God with regard to the children of believing parents in its reflection of church, home, and school (John 21:15–17[9]; see also Deuteronomy 6:1–15; Psalm 78). Also pictured is proactive obedience to God's command regarding those "afar off, as many as the Lord will call" (see discussion in chapters 3 and 4). Most important, the model represents a renewed way

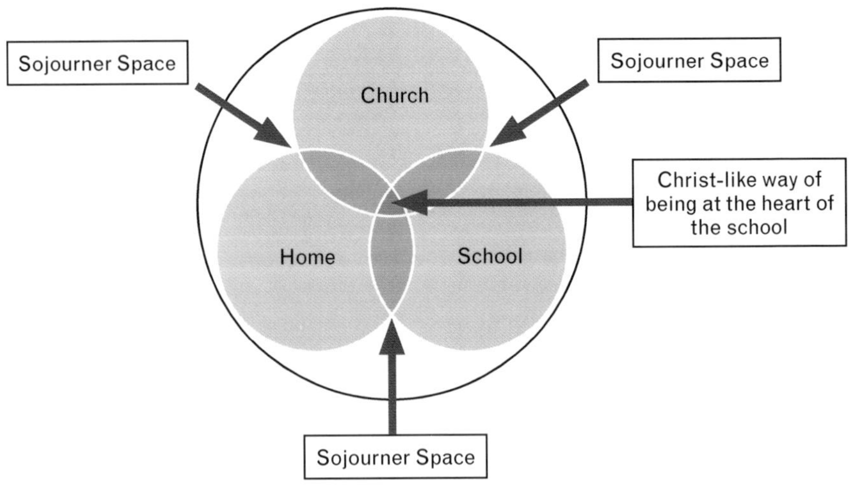

Graciously Unapologetic Christian School Model

of being at the heart of a school. Ideally it provides a structure in which to reflect Christ *in His way of being*, without the need for fear-driven artificial controls.

I wonder whether Peter thoroughly confused those Jews who listened to the first New Testament sermon by his conclusion: "the promise is to you and to your children *and to those afar off, as many as the Lord will call*" (Acts 2:39, emphasis mine). This should not have been perplexing; God had widely taught the "far off" concept throughout the Old Testament. But it was. Fear drove the lovers of self-righteousness and controllers of salvation, which in turn drew the rebukes of the New Testament epistles. Are those rebukes applicable to *this* ensuing generation? Have controls originated from reaction to fears held by Christians entrusted with the responsibility of forming and leading Christian schools? If this is not the case, then what model, policy, or ways of being are in place to allow *both* the children of believers and of those "afar off" to approach the promise of Christ *without seeking control* of God's kingdom building and soul saving?

God works in the line of generations and does certainly call some from "afar off"; that much is clear from verse 39. My question is this: "What is obedient and lovingly proactive toward God when a desire to 'get near' is in evidence?" I could repeat several traditional answers to that question, but each of them would allow for forms of control highly unlike Christ's way of being. Is it possible to obey God's commands to simultaneously "teach Christ" to children of believers and to "those afar off," while trusting God with the sovereign means to move people, far and near, as He wills? I contend that to do so without fear and controls is obedient, not simply justifiable.

"The fear of the LORD [and only of the LORD] is the beginning of wisdom" (Proverbs 9:10); every realm of the Christian life derives its meaning and objective from that underlying conviction. Learning that offers more than temporal utility is rooted in the full revelation of Jesus Christ (Colossians 1:16–17),[10] implying that this full revelation is to be integrated into all learning as the final and absolute authority on all matters of faith and life. Consider a scenario in which the full revelation is integrated into all learning *and* a Christ-like way of being is consistently reflected and passionately pursued in every organizational and relational application. Such a setting would certainly minimize fear and control by ensuring that content and process are about a proactive reflection of Christ rather than a reactive reflection of what is feared.

The New Testament Gentiles who were drawn from "afar off" did not all enter the religious community of the Jews with a full understanding of God's work. Many who desired fellowship did not do so for pure reasons. Some walked away after a time, others maintained a peaceful coexistence, and still others were drawn all the way into the promise through regeneration. My point is not that Christian schools should or will or can—or shouldn't or won't or can't—save anyone; I frankly don't believe that it's the business of the Christian school to identify as objectives of its work salvific production, identification, or isolation. The objective of the Christian school is to *teach Christ* in content and process, trusting *God* with the faith and the saving. The critical question is this: Have Christian schools been faithful in teaching Christ alone in both content and process?

Imagine that someone who is "afar off" asks permission to attend church services or a home Bible study, agreeing to follow the guidelines of that church or home, but is denied access. The outsider is being denied access to the promise (Christ) *by one who has confessed to having been saved by Grace and, as a result, entirely of Christ, is walking in Truth*. The confessional content and living process reflected in this scenario are deeply incongruent. Yet Christian schools are widely modeled and organized on this very lack of congruence.

Now imagine that children of believers *and* of those from "afar off" are jointly attending services and Bible study; those who are following the rules are pronounced "saved," while those who are not are urged to "get saved" by following those rules. The very pronouncement implies, from the mouth of *one who has confessed to having been saved by Grace and, as a result, entirely of Christ, is walking in Truth*, that outward acts earn God's application of the promise (Christ). The confessional content and living process are deeply incongruent. Yet Christian schools are widely modeled and organized on this incongruence.

Is Christian education as a whole in crisis because too few people are attracted to congruent teaching of Christ? Maybe. It's more likely, though, that many who are attracted to talk of Christ are at the same time repelled by an inconsistent walk on the part of those who profess Him. Or they hear truth but miss out on meaningful applications of grace. Or they receive grace but hear little truth. Or they hear a strong tradition but a weak testimony. Or they turn away because Christian school leaders are straining at gnats but swallowing camels (Matthew 23:23–24).[11] Certainly there is no one definitive answer except to say that Christian schools are suffering from widespread spiritual dysfunction. May God grant a way to unity through renewal to a Christ-like way of being.

Astounding spiritual renewal will come to the school community that is serious about a reflection of Christ in His way of being, while modeled to obey the command of God to teach Christ in content and process to the children of believers *and* to those from afar off, as many as the Lord will call (to sojourners). Consequences include teaching that is renewed both by believing *and by living belief proactively*; by reflecting Christ, *whether easy or difficult*; and by being transparent, accountable, and vulnerable, *whether self-incriminating or not*. The life of a school, if Christian in more than name, is dependent upon lovingly and proactively reflecting the gracious and unapologetic life of Christ, while trusting God with the results.

"According to the grace of God which was given to me as a wise master builder, I have laid the foundation, and others build on that foundation. But let every man pay attention how he builds on that foundation. For no other foundation can be laid by men than that which has been laid in Jesus Christ." (1 Corinthians 3:10–11)

3

What Is a Sojourner?

"Also, you may not oppress a sojourner: because you know the heart of a sojourner, because you were sojourners in the land of Egypt." (Exodus 23:9)

The word "sojourner" has been chosen for use in this book to identify a group of people who bear a unique relationship to the covenant community throughout the Old and New Testaments. English versions of the Bible interchangeably translate the relevant Hebrew and Greek words as "sojourner," "stranger," "foreigner," and/or "alien." The Hebrew and Greek words relevant to identification of this particular subset of Gentiles (sojourners) are found in the table on page 16. (Lexicon) (Interlinear Bible)

"Sojourner(s)" is not a synonym for "unbeliever(s)," just as "Israelite(s)" and/or "church member(s)" are not synonyms for "believer(s)." A sojourner begins "afar off" from the word of promise, while the child of a believer begins near to the word of promise. Believers have *entered into* (as opposed to being near to or far away from) the word of promise through Christ alone (Romans 9:6–8).[1] Sojourners are a subset of all those who are "afar off." The subset consists of "as many as the Lord shall call." With application to sojourners, God commands that His covenant people share all blessings and apply all

Word	Greek or Hebrew Lexicon Definition: KJV
ger, guwr *Hebrew*	– a temporary inhabitant, a newcomer lacking inherited rights of foreigners in Israel, though possessing conceded rights (noun) – to sojourn, abide, dwell in, dwell with, remain, inhabit, be a stranger, be continuing, dwell for a time, to abide, stay, temporarily dwell, to seek hospitality with, to assemble oneself (verb)
towshab *Hebrew*	– stranger, sojourner (noun) – Ancient word origin Yashab: to dwell, remain, sit, abide; or cause to sit, abide, dwell, be inhabited; or make dwell (verb)
xenos *Greek*	– a foreigner, a stranger, alienated from a person or thing, without knowledge of or share in, one who receives hospitality where he stays or lodges
paraikos, paroikeo *Greek*	– a stranger, a foreigner, living without rights of citizenship; a metaphor for one who lives with citizenship in God's kingdom, on earth as stranger, home is heaven (noun) – to dwell beside or in one's neighborhood, to live near, to be or dwell in a place as a stranger, to sojourn (verb)
epidemeo, parepidemos *Greek*	– of a foreign resident, among any people, in any country – one who comes from a foreign country into a city or land to reside there by the side of the natives, a stranger sojourning in a strange place, a foreigner, one who sojourns on earth

legal consequences and protection, while excluding from the sacraments and leadership (chapter 4).

The characteristics of a sojourner are:

1. living out of the native element, physically or spiritually; possessing no inherited right.
2. aware of need and/or dependence, either physically or spiritually.
3. seeking, and willing to enter, mutually responsible association.

The concept of sojourner is used in the Bible in two different physical pictures that teach of two distinct spiritual realities. First, Adam is thrust from his native element, barred from the garden of Eden to sojourn, as one cursed, on the cursed earth. The rights inherited as an image-bearer and friend of the Creator have been lost. All humankind in Adam is spiritually dead, but a subset is restored to fellowship with God through Christ and receives His inherited rights in eternal life. Second, "sojourn" is used to describe the physical life of those who have been restored to fellowship with God; people who have been reborn from above (John 3:3).[2] Each "new creation" in Christ (2 Corinthians 5:17)[3] is living in the world, displaced from his (new) native element of citizenship and rights in heaven.

The Bible also speaks a great deal about sojourning to describe people in a particular circumstance. It is this circumstance with which this book primarily deals. A person on the earth is displaced by, or discomforted with, his native element. This person finds himself living among, or coming into contact with, other natives of the earth while having no inherited right to fellowship there. If/when covenant people live among or come into contact with those outside the covenant community, God specifies that covenant people are to interact with the sojourner(s) in a way that reflects God's relational interaction with believers. In this way the sojourner comes near to the Word of promise and is exposed to content, but also to a way of being (process) that reflects God's relationship with His people. God does whatever He wills in that circumstance.

As you will see in this chapter and the next, God makes a big point of progressive instruction on the concept of sojourners. "For the LORD your God is God of gods, and LORD of lords, a great God, a mighty, and a terrible, that regards not persons, nor takes a reward: He executes judgment of the fatherless and widow, and loves the sojourner (*ger*), in giving him food and raiment. You therefore love the sojourner (*ger*): for you were sojourners (*ger*) in the land of Egypt" (Deuteronomy 10:17–19, paraphrase mine).

Instruction on sojourners begins with the first hint of God's promise, the coming of Christ (Genesis 3:15), after Adam is expelled from the garden (verses 23–24). Friendship with God could not be restored without the promise (Christ). Not long afterward God gives more instruction on how restored friendship is to be accomplished. He commands Abram to leave his land, people, and family and to wander around among foreigners (12:1), all the while trusting God's promise of a permanent home. Later on God informs Abram: "[C]ertain of your offspring will be sojourners (*ger*) in a land that is not theirs and will be servants there, and they will be afflicted for four hundred years" (15:13). The sojourn of these descendants in Egypt and their subsequent exodus comprise progressive revelation on the bondage to sin and liberation through the blood of the Lamb (Exodus 12; 1 Corinthians 5:7–8). Again and again God returns to the sojourn of Abram, and to the Israelites in Egypt, as the basis for His commands about the treatment of *ger* among His covenant people.

Jacob hosted sojourners: "Jacob said to his household [*bayith*: household, those belonging to the same household], and to all that were with him, put away the strange (*nekar*: foreign, alien, vain) gods that are among you, and be clean, and change your garments: Let us arise and go to Beth-el; and I will make there an altar to God, who answered me in my distress, and was with me in the way that I went" (Genesis 35:2–3). Jacob's experience teaches in both content and process about the one true God; he does not bar the idolatrous sojourners from his home, fellowship, tents, or worship. Jacob buried the idols but did not prohibit the sojourners from continuing to dwell in his household.

In the exodus Jacob's descendants, too, hosted sojourners as they traveled out of Egypt: "and a mixed (*ereb*: mixture, mixed company, mixed people) multitude (*rab*: much, many, great) went up also with them" (Exodus 12:38a). When Moses gave the law (20:10[4]; see also Deuteronomy 5:14), sojourners continued to dwell within the fellowship and company of Israel. Speaking of Sabbath rest from labors, God is inclusive, specifying, ". . . nor the sojourner (*ger*) that is within your gates."

Later on in biblical history sojourners continued to live in mutually responsible association with Israel. Speaking of God's people, David confessed in prayer, "For we are strangers (*ger*) before You, and sojourners (*towshab*), as were all our fathers: our days on the earth are as a shadow, and there is none abiding" (1 Chronicles 29:15). David assigned sojourners (*ger*) to take part in building the temple (22:2),[5] and Solomon later counted 153,600 sojourners (*ger*) and gave them occupations in temple building. Some were menial laborers, some stone artisans, and others managers (2 Chronicles 2:17–18).[6]

Speaking inclusively of all foreigners, Solomon prayed, "Also concerning the stranger (*nokriy*: foreign, alien) who is not of Your people Israel, when he comes from a far country for Your name's sake, because they will hear of Your great name and Your mighty hand, and of Your outstretched arm; when he comes and prays toward this house, hear in heaven Your dwelling place, and do according to all for which the foreigner (*nokriy*: foreign, alien) calls to You, in order that all the people of the earth may know Your name, to fear You, as do Your people Israel, and that they may know that this house that I have built is called by Your name" (1 Kings 8:41–43). Solomon's prayer was that foreigners (*nokriy*) would be drawn near and live as *ger*. From Pentecost through today this prayer of Solomon is being answered. What are Christian schools doing with the *ger*?

Solomon's porch, and the corresponding porch in later temple rebuilding, was a common place of reception for sojourners (*ger*), beggars, the lame, and other needy persons (6:3, 2 Chronicles 3:4). The porch was also the site of Jesus' healing of a lame man who had been waiting for an angel to stir the waters (John 5:1–9). After Jesus' ascension the porch became an integral meeting point for the preaching of the gospel, powerfully signifying the destruction of the "middle wall of partition" between Gentiles (those spiritually afar off) and Jews (those near to Christ) (Acts 3:11; 5:12).[7]

The height of the temple porch was four times that of other temple parts (compare 1 Kings 6:2, 20 with 2 Chronicles 3:4), intentionally built to attract *nokriy* to draw near as *ger*. The porch typified the light of Christ that would be shed abroad into the world. Still today the charity of a biblical faith community will shed light all around and attract as many sojourners as the Lord will call. "Do not forget to entertain strangers (*philoxenia*: love to strangers, hospitality)" (Hebrews 13:2a), and be "given to hospitality (*philoxenia*)" (Romans 12:13b).

God was so serious about the extension of fellowship and rights to circumstantial sojourners that the prophets used this image to describe a time of spiritual health: "[Y]ou will divide it by lot for an inheritance to you, and to the sojourners (*ger*) that sojourn (*guwr*) among you, that have beget children among you: ***and they will be to you as born in the country among the children of Israel***; they will have ***inheritance*** with you among the tribes of Israel. And it will come to pass, that in what tribe the sojourner (*ger*) sojourns (*guwr*), there will you give him his inheritance, saith the Lord God" (Ezekiel 47:21–23, paraphrase mine).

While considering the bold, italicized words above, consider a summary (mine) of Deuteronomy 6:7–12, which in recent history has been primarily used to justify the **exclusion** of the children of sojourners: "Teach your children the words of God diligently, talk of them when you sit in your house, walk by the way, lie down, and rise up. Bind them for a sign on your hand and as frontlets between your eyes. Write them on the posts of your house and on your gates. And when you come to the land that I promised you, whose blessings you did nothing to receive, beware in case you forget the LORD, the one who brought you out of your slavery to live with Him ***(and they will be to you as born in the country among the children of Israel).***" (See also 11:18–22.)

The oppression of the sojourner, either by active harm or through passive response to need, was so serious that God instructed in Exodus 22:21, "[D]o not vex (*yanah*: oppress, suppress, treat violently, maltreat, vex, do wrong) a sojourner (*ger*), nor oppress him: for you were sojourners (*ger*) in the land of Egypt" (KJV). In verses 22–24 God goes on to say in effect (paraphrase mine), "If you do so and they (sojourner, widow, fatherless) cry at all to me, I will surely hear their cry; and my anger will wax hot, and I will kill you with the sword; and your wives will be widows, and your children fatherless."

In part, exile was a consequence of failure to obey commands about sojourners and other weaker members of the community. In Zechariah 7:9–14 the prophet puts it like this: "This is what God said: administer true justice; show mercy and compassion to each other. Do not oppress the widow, fatherless, sojourner (*ger*), or the poor. Do not plot evil against each other. But they refused to pay attention, stubbornly they turned their backs and covered their ears. They made their hearts as hard as flint and would not listen to the law or the words that God sent by his Spirit through earlier prophets. So God was very angry. When I called, they didn't listen; so when they called, I didn't listen, says God. I scattered them with a whirlwind among the nations, where they became sojourners among the nations whom they knew not. The land they left behind is desolate and no one travels through it. This is how they made the pleasant land desolate" (paraphrase mine).

Malachi, prophesying of the messenger who will prepare the way for Christ, says, "And I will come near to you in judgment; and I will be a swift witness . . . against those that turn aside the sojourner (*ger*) from his right, and do not fear me, says the LORD of hosts" (Malachi 3:5, paraphrase mine). As foretold, Jesus entered the world as a sojourner and identified Himself with sojourners: "I was a sojourner (*xenos*), and you took me in" (Mathew 25:35b). Christ left heaven (his native element) to earn citizenship for sinners in the city of God, and in His ministry Christ makes fellowship with sojourners (*xenos*) a litmus test for true spirituality (verses 4–43).

During His earthly sojourn Jesus extended fellowship to all those who drew near. For example, in 13:13–21 Jesus taught (and fed) the entire crowd. And in Luke 17:11–19 He healed ten lepers, only one (*allogenes*, of another tribe or nation) of whom received the power to believe. Our Lord did not withhold the teaching of truth or the physical signs of His spiritual work from any who would draw near. Following the instruction of Jesus, people either continued to follow or they did not continue to follow.

Speaking to believers in Ephesus, Paul says in effect, "You've seen the sojourner, and he is you. You were without Christ, aliens (*apallotrioo*, shut out from fellowship and intimacy) from the nation of Israel, and sojourners (*xenos*, without knowledge or share in) from the covenants of promise, without hope, and without God: now in Christ Jesus you who were afar off have been brought near by the blood of Christ. He is our peace and has made us both one, taking down the wall of partition between us. . . . And he came and preached peace to you that were afar off, and to them that were near" (Ephesians 2:12–17, paraphrase mine).

Jesus Christ says, "[T]he righteous (sheep) will answer, 'Lord, when did we see you as a sojourner (*xenos*) and we took you in?' And the King will answer, 'when you did it to the least of my brothers you did it to me.' And those on the left (goats) will answer, 'when did we see you a sojourner (*xenos*) and didn't take you in?' Then the King answered, 'Truly, when you didn't do it to the least, you didn't do it to me'" (Matthew 25:31–46, paraphrase mine).

God has always taught about sojourners/sojourning: "For these all died in faith, not having received the things promised, but having seen them and greeted them from afar, and having acknowledged that they were sojourners (*xenos*) and exiles (*parepedimos*) on the earth" (Hebrews 11:13, KJV). God has stressed a point about the relationship between believers and sojourners from beginning to end. I could, of course, be wrong in my own conclusions about what His point is and how it is to be applied. But the questions remain, crying out for answers: What *is* the point and how *is* it to be applied? In Christian schools the issue seems primarily to have either been ignored or, at best, poorly tolerated.

> "Beloved, you do faithfully whatever you are doing to the brethren, and to the sojourners (*xenos*); who have given testimony of your love." (3 John 1:5–6a, paraphrase mine)

4

Boundaries and Blessings

At least four points are clear. First, Christ was a sojourner in human flesh and in that state earned heavenly citizenship for sinners. Second, the Christian community is called to reflect Christ to the sojourners of earth, as host. Third, fellowship with sojourners is a litmus test for true spirituality. And fourth, the pattern of Christian community is designed by God to attract some from "afar off, as many as the Lord will call" to come near.

There are two biblical mandates that limit the bounds of a sojourner within the community of faith, and only one of those has functional rather than instructive application to the Christian school. The first mandate is exclusion from leadership, and the second is exclusion from the sacraments. In all other respects boundaries relating to all people residing in a biblical faith community are identical. All share in the blessing, all submit to law in terms of consequence and protection, and any may be expelled or removed.

Before continuing, it will be helpful to distinguish the meanings of some additional Greek and Hebrew words that do not refer to sojourn or sojourners as we are using the terms in this book but that are also interchangeably translated into the English Bible text as "sojourner," "stranger," "foreigner," and/or "alien." The following explanation may avoid some confusion, should some wish to study the concepts further.

The word *zuwr* takes its unique meaning from the context in which it is used. In Numbers 16:40 it means "anyone not of Aaron's blood," in 1:51 "anyone that is not a Levite," and in Deuteronomy 25:5 "anyone from another family." Leviticus 22:10 uses *zuwr* to contrast priests with non-priests, while the distinction in Exodus 30:9 is between holy and profane.

The words *nokhri* and *ben nekhar* are widely used throughout the Old Testament as general terms, in a variety of contexts, for any foreigner. As God's plan approaches ever nearer to the incarnation of Christ, the prophets increasingly speak of foreigners from all nations (*nokhri and ben nekhar)* being drawn near to the promise. The prophet Isaiah in Isaiah 56:1 states, "my salvation is near to come, and my righteousness to be revealed." In verse 3 he goes on to exhort, "Don't let the stranger (*nekhar*) say the LORD has separated me from His people," and in verse 6 he declares that "the sons of the stranger (*nekhar*) that love the LORD are His servants and take hold of the covenant (promise); them will I bring to my Holy mountain . . . for my house will be called an house of prayer for all peoples" (paraphrase mine). The Old Testament *ger* prefigured the Pentecost calling of *ben nekhar* from every nation to come near to the blood of Christ as *ger.*

Hebrew/Greek Word	Definition
Zuwr *Hebrew*	– to be strange, a stranger, estranged, alienated, a foreign enemy, loathsome, alienated
Nokhri or Ben Nekhar *Hebrew*	– foreign, alien, foreignness, that which is foreign, foreign gods, alien, foreigner foreign (vanities)
allotrios or apallotrioo *Greek*	– belonging to another

The fulfillment of these prophecies is seen, in part, in the use of *allotrios* and *apallotrioo* in Ephesians 2:12 (see also Colossians 1:21, where Paul states that "you were without Christ, being aliens (*apallotrioo*)." This particular passage reminded the Gentile sojourners at Ephesus that they had been far away and had belonged to another. God had brought them near to the promise "by the blood of Christ" (verse 13). Someone may have evangelized them, or God may have drawn them into sojourn by some other means.

Paul prays that the Ephesus group might receive wisdom, revelation, enlightened understanding, knowledge of hope, and Christ's inheritance and power (Ephesians 1:15–23). His prayer exposes his assumption that regeneration had not necessarily preceded sojourn. And yet Paul greets and receives each (verses 1–2) as "home born," much as one would hope the pastor would do in corporate prayer. Or the teacher in the classroom. Or the parent with children.

Christian schools pursue mission compliance through a variety of grand ideals, all with the stated objective of bringing glory to God. While we are "doing" all of the stuff to chase these self-assigned ideals that God has in reality assigned to Himself, has our sense of "being" confident in Christ alone and fearless in testimony been lost? Because if "confident in Christ" and "fearless in testimony" had been a way of being, a fear of sojourners would not have necessitated artificial controls designed to protect self-assigned ideals. "What shall we do?" is a vain question, in terms of spiritual authenticity, when "who are we to be?" has been forgotten.

Boundary #1: Exclusion from Leadership

God speaks about leadership among His people with unyielding clarity. The leader in the Christian community reflects the roles of Christ as Prophet, Priest, and King. In the Old Testament the law looks forward with belief to Christ's righteousness and sacrifice, while in the New we are convicted by the Spirit in the heart, living in the realization of Christ's completed work (Ezekiel 36:26).

All those holding organizationally sanctioned oversight in the Christian community must be qualified by demonstrable and long-standing testimony of faith in Jesus Christ. (Yes, of course, they must *also* be skilled for the work.) The exclusion from leadership in the Christian school pertains to all foreigners, including the subset referred to in this book as sojourners, and it sets a high evidentiary standard for professed believers who are obtaining and continuing in leadership within the Christian community.

As fear builds constructs of control to protect the kingdom or save souls, members of a community perceive themselves to be spiritually safe. Within that false security, accountability measured by the unyielding standard of Christ wanes, while traditional norms wax as the measure of spiritual fitness for leadership. Naturally, such a crew thinks themselves to be "steering" the ship while they are in reality drifting far and wide from the charted course. If the reader has spent considerable time in Christian education, he or she might find it instructive to ponder the number of persons retaining positions of leadership in the Christian school with respect to whom "nice" and "good" are the only descriptors of spiritual functionality that come to mind.

So *no*, do not set those *far* or even *near* to Jesus Christ in positions of leadership in the Christian school. But *yes*, do implement and maintain daily, authentic, relational accountability standards for leaders to reflect that they are growing *in* Christ as the standard of measurement for those in leadership roles in the Christian school. I would posit that low standards of spirituality for leadership have been a far greater problem for Christian education in recent decades than the challenges of a rapidly changing world. If leaders are not growing *in* Christ, the school will die. Whether or not it dies organizationally only God can say; but spiritually it will certainly die. A *form* of godliness cannot maintain spiritual life without the *power* thereof. From mere forms one must actively turn away (2 Timothy 3:5).

"You will always set a ruler over you that the LORD your God has chosen: one from among your brethren will you set to rule over you; you may not set a stranger (*'iysh: human being, mankind, great man, champion, whosoever*) to rule over you, that is not your brother (*ach: relative, kinship, same tribe*)" (Deuteronomy 17:15, paraphrase mine). See also Exodus 18:21, Luke 22:25–27, Acts 20:28, Ephesians 4:11–16, 1 Timothy 3:1–18, 2 Timothy 2:15, Titus 1:5–9, James 3:1, and 1 Peter 5:3.

Boundary #2: Exclusion from Sacraments

Since the sacraments of the Lord's Supper and Baptism (the New Testament covenant manifestations of Passover and circumcision) are appropriately administered in the church, this exclusion is instructive rather than organizationally functional for the school. In Exodus 12:43–48 God dictates to Moses and Aaron the rules for the first Passover meal. In verse 43 God specifies that "no foreigner (*ben nekhar*) may eat it," and in verses 45 and 48, respectively, He declares that "the temporary resident" (*towshab*) and "the foreigner residing among you" (*ger)* may not eat unless all of the males in his household have first been circumcised.

God recognizes three distinct groups in this passage: foreigners (*ben nekhar*), temporary sojourners (*towshab*), and more permanent sojourners (*ger)*. None of them were permitted to eat the Passover meal unless they had first received the sign and seal of the covenant through circumcision.

This passage is instructive for the Christian school because it exposes what is assumed: that the sojourner is qualified for fellowship within the fabric of covenant life even *without* the precondition of religious observance. In fact, sojourners at the time of the exodus were sheltered to the extent that they left Egypt with Israel (in a mixed multitude) *without having participated in the Passover meal.* Given the spiritual reality to which the Passover points (see Exodus 12 and 1 Corinthians 5:7–8), that shelter reflected astounding grace played out unapologetically.

Suppose that in 40 years of wandering the first generation of Israelites had taught the wonderful works of the Lord to the second. Were the children of sojourners within this mixed multitude wandering the desert with Israel learning at a different school because they had not taken part in Passover and/or circumcision?

Boundary #3: Open Opposition

Perhaps the most difficult boundary to maintain, for all members of a community led by biblical faith, is the line that must be drawn when active and open opposition forces a nonnegotiable stance. When biblically legitimate, the high cost and deep sorrow of separation become very personal for believing leaders. The quiet resolution of "Here I stand; God help me, I can do no other" is wrung from the gracious soul that has "borne all things, hoped all things, believed all things, and endured all things" (1 Corinthians 13:7) for the sake of the most excellent way (12:31), reflecting Christ's love *even when* the only remaining way is through separation.

Consider Psalm 146:9: "The LORD preserves the sojourners (*ger*); he relieves the fatherless and widow: but the way of the wicked (*rasha'*, *openly hostile to God*) He turns upside down" (paraphrase mine).

God is not squeamish about this. But humans fear to stand where the only remaining course of loving action is separation. Taking this stand is itself exceedingly gracious and truthful. However, it requires spiritual strength and courage; the qualities of "nice" and "good" will be of no assistance at such a time. Fear of bearing that cross can cause a desire to manage for particular outcomes, and a number of alternative controls may be invented to avoid the nonnegotiable stand. These controls are falsely perceived to provide safety—or, more damaging, "peace."

Openly and actively oppositional people do sovereignly comingle with, or rise up within, Christian churches, schools, and families (note 2 Timothy 3). It is not faith but fear that results in artificial controls to protect from this possible eventuality. Not only are these controls faithless, they are ineffective; they do not reflect a biblical Christ and will not protect the community from open opposition. When open and active opposition does arise from inside or outside a faith community, once its leaders have expended all efforts and have yielded wherever possible, God Himself will uphold and defend (4:14–18).

The law of many lands, including those in North America, allow for the removal of parties that fail to meet the communicated expectations of a faith-based (or other) community, *provided the admission and interaction take place without prequalifying discrimination.* The fact is that the vast majority of opposition in Christian schools is realized passively in spiritual dysfunction that hides behind the "nice" and "good" behavior of professed believers and their children. Passively opposed participants most often walk away on their own (1 John 2:19) or hang around to enjoy community benefits as noncombative participants in outward ceremony (Matthew 13:25–30).

Boundary #4: The Sharing of Blessings

Believers live in restored friendship with God because, in Christ, unmerited favor is maintained toward them. But at one time they had been sojourners, thrust out of Eden along with Adam. God did what was needed *in His own being* so that believers are able to live at His place and share the fellowship of friendship with Him. And He maintains this favor *during and in spite of* residual sin. God will continue His good work of salvation in the believer until it is complete through the indwelling of the Master Teacher (Philippians 1:6).

So when God says to former sojourners, such as leaders in Christian education, "I wasn't partial about saving you and I can't be bribed. I execute justice for all kinds of helpless people and therefore love the sojourner, because that's what you are to me" (Deuteronomy 10:17–19, paraphrase mine), I think one should assume this demands some *demonstrable reflection of Christ's grace and truth in every facet of the faith-based community, including relationships with sojourners.*

Again, the question at issue for Christian schools is "what is obedient and lovingly proactive when a sojourner's desire to 'get near' is in evidence?" Or, expressed another way, how much of the blessing that has been received by the believer is to be shared? The unequivocal answer: *all that has been received.* "Rejoice in all the blessings that the Lord has given you, and the Levite, and the sojourner (*ger*). And when you have finished tithing from all your blessings to the Levite, sojourner, fatherless, and widow, so that they share in all your blessings *in your house*, then you will be able to say to Me that you have kept my commandments and have not transgressed or forgotten them" (Deuteronomy 26:11–13, paraphrase mine).

Following are specific examples of the instruction to share blessings. Sojourners are: allowed foods forbidden to Israelites (14:21); provided for along with the fatherless and the widows (24:17–22); to receive the benefit of the tithe (14:28–29); to work within the economy of Israel (29:10–15); in terms of their descendants, to enjoy full entrance into the nation (23:7–8)[1]; to participate in assembly and Feasts (Joshua 8:30–35[2]; see also Deuteronomy 29:10–13; 16:10–11, 13–14); to make offerings (Numbers 15:14–15)[3]; and, when describing a time of spiritual health, permitted by God to have their children treated as home-born (Ezekiel 47:21–23).[4]

God makes a promise to Abraham in Genesis 12:3 that through him all the families of the earth will be blessed. Isaiah underscores this promise by expounding on the purpose of God to draw *nekhar* from every nation on the earth to become *ger*. The prophet foresaw that people from every nation in the world would be able to give themselves the surname of Israel (Isaiah 44:5) and that Christ would bring justice to the heretofore marginalized Gentiles (42:1–4), that He would be a light to the Gentiles to the end of the earth (49:6), and that nations that did not know Him would run to Him (55:4–5).

I am quite certain that leaders in the Christian school have a cognitive knowledge of all that the Old Testament mentions about the purposes of God in the coming of Christ. What I am wondering is how this particular work of His is *reflected* in a way of being when God calls "afar off" Gentiles to desire sojourn near to Christ in the Christian school.

Boundary #5: The Protection and Consequence of Law

The protection and consequence of law are blessings that are to be completely shared. Numbers 15:15–16 stipulates that "one ordinance will apply to both the home-born and the sojourner (*ger*). As it is for the home-born, so will it be for the sojourner (*ger*). One law and one application will be for the both" (paraphrase mine). The same instruction is repeated in Exodus 12:49[5] and in Leviticus 17:15 and 24:22.

The biblical instruction on law includes an equitable share as well in terms of consequences. Leviticus 24:16 instructs that "him that blasphemes the name of the LORD, he will be put to death for sure, and all the congregation will have to stone him. The same for the sojourner (*ger*) and him that is born in the land: when he blasphemes the name of the LORD, he will be put to death" (paraphrase mine).

Interestingly, the predominant instruction consists of warnings to Israelites not to *pervert* the law *against* the "ger." Even after having received God's mercy, Israel tended toward prejudicial and discriminatory use of legal protection and consequence when it came to sojourners. God's intention of loving discipline based on His law (discipleship) was perverted to express and apply the discriminatory hatred of men—not the gracious consequences that reflect the justice and mercy of God in Christ.

History proves again and again that there is indeed nothing new under the sun (Ecclesiastes 1:9). One might rationalize the tendency to pervert legal protection and consequence on the part of Old Testament believers who had not yet seen the fulfillment of the law in Christ. They lived, after all, under a very heavy burden. The relief of Simeon is almost palpable when He fixes his gaze on the newborn Christ and enthuses, "Let your servant depart in peace . . . I have seen Your salvation . . . a light of revelation to the Gentiles, and the glory of Your people" (Luke 2:29–32, paraphrase mine).

But what excuse is there for those of us living in the freedom of Christ's completed work? Is it worth considering whether "kingdom building" is an excuse for a perversion of law that prevents sojourners from being present in the faith community? Or if "soul saving" is an excuse for perverting the law within a faith community, where law becomes the measure of a righteousness that "proves" salvation? And further, whether either of these perversions might be the result of our fears that Christ *alone* has not, or cannot, fully accomplish His own work.

The ominous warnings of the Word against the perversion of law against the sojourner (and others in need) are many. The psalmist prays that the wicked *among God's people* will be judged for slaying the "ger" (Psalm 94:6).[6] A "ger" is not to be overworked or underpaid and must not be kept from gleaning in the field, under the olive tree, or along the grapevine (Deuteronomy 24:19–22).[7] Righteousness and judgment must be executed on behalf of the "ger" and the offender judged (Jeremiah 22:3).[8] Failure to execute justice on behalf of the sojourner is one of the symptoms of spiritual disease that resulted in the desolation of Israel described in Jeremiah 5. In several instances—as in Malachi 3:5[9]—God promises to appear in judgment when the right of the "ger" is turned aside. Leaders are charged to judge righteously between every man and "ger" (Deuteronomy 1:16).[10] And when the "ger" feels oppressed and cries out to God, the sin is charged to the Israelite oppressor (24:14–15).[11]

> "You should not pervert the judgment of the sojourner (*ger*) . . . but you *should* remember that you were a slave in Egypt, and the LORD your God redeemed you from there: that's *why* I command you to do this" (Deuteronomy 24:17–18, paraphrase mine).

Conclusion

> "Do not forget to entertain strangers (*philoxenia: love to strangers, sojourners, hospitality*)" (Hebrews 13:2a), and be "given to hospitality (*philoxenia: love to strangers, sojourners, hospitality*)" (Romans 12:13b).

A Christian school is not called to transform lives, build the kingdom, change the world, win souls, or eradicate the effects of the fall. *God does all of that in His own good pleasure.* Rather, the people of God are called to obedience: to *teach Christ,* rooted in a restored and loving friendship with God, through the power and way of Christ alone. That God uses obedience in teaching Christ alone as His chosen means to the ends of His good pleasure is obvious. But His designated *way* to His end is obedience. Have God's ends been hijacked as Christian school ends, consequently blurring God's big point about His way of obedience? Christian schools *do* many things to meet their self-assigned mission statement ends. But are those things obediently reflective of Christ's graciously unapologetic way of being in His earthly sojourn toward the children of believers and also of those who are "afar off"?

> "And Jesus said, 'No, in case while you are pulling up weeds, you also pull up the wheat with them. Let them both grow together until the harvest: and in the time of harvest I will say to the reapers, first gather together the weeds, and bind them together in bundles to burn them: but gather the wheat into my barn.'" (Matthew 13:29–30)

5

Some Objections to Enrolling the Children of Sojourners Addressed

If one has objections to including space in the Christian school for the children of sojourners, they might find some of them briefly discussed in this chapter. I don't know all of the objections, of course, or have all the answers. However, I have wrestled in the direction of my now confident position ever since I was in the sixth grade. This has been a significant departure from my inherited tradition, and the issue has occupied my careful thoughts on the subject of renewal for a very long time. Regardless of which Christian school model one might be—or have been—bound to, I am convinced that Christian education is in need of spiritual renewal, in need of a unified, obedient commitment to *one* objective and *one* mission for the work: *to teach Christ in all content and process to both the children of believers and to those of individuals who are afar off.*

I suspect that my thoughts on the matter began in the sixth grade when I broached the following with my dad: "Why is Jane Doe allowed to go to our school? No one in her family goes to church." I didn't ask on the basis of

Jane's enrollment bothering me or as a sign of any particular spiritual depth in myself. Quite the opposite. Jane was my nice little sixth-grade friend. I simply asked because I noticed that her enrollment was inconsistent with the stated policy, with the accepted and understood way of being in my church and school. And I didn't want to lose her as a friend.

My dad had a way of steering me toward deeper reflection. He responded, "Because God brought her. You live what you believe. God will do what God pleases." Sensing his evasion, and perhaps his disagreement with the policy, I probed, "But do you *agree* with it?" "I agree." he replied, deliberately evasive in a way that invited broader insight, "that when we are faithful, it doesn't matter. The important question is: are we faithful?" My father was a minister in the Christian Reformed Church, the year was 1973, and the school was Timothy Christian in Rexdale, Ontario, Canada.

Much later, while working in Christian schools, I came to realize just how it was that Jane had gotten in. She had gained access in the same way "they" often do it today: as someone's grandchild; based on the influence of money; by someone's willingness to lie; through a policy loophole; on account of possessing the right complement of outward qualifiers; or as an oversight. A more recent addition to the "ways in" is through open preschool admissions policies (no one is afraid of three- and four-year-old sinners) in the same school in which K–12 admissions policies prequalify by artificial constructs of control. Preschool provides the family some needed time to meet prequalifying standards—not to mention that the revenue is highly appreciated.

The children of sojourners are not *entirely* missing from Christian schools; they "slip in" and are tolerated or even pronounced "saved" if they are well behaved. But the predominant means of their entrance into and continuation in Christian schools is meeting the pre- and/or post-qualifying measurements designed to determine Christian "fitness." My primary objection to this is that "they" rarely get in, or are permitted to stay, as the result of honest, truth-filled conversations and graciously unapologetic relationships. I'll be the first to admit feeling "holy" when I have "tolerated" the sovereign acts of God that have allowed "them" to slip in, labeling my tolerance as grace. I'm suggesting a need for spiritual renewal that welcomes rather than tolerates the sovereign acts of God as He moves people from "far" to "near," while trusting Him with the controls. And that also embraces, rather than rejects, the directive for authentic, Christ-like covenantal communities where the sojourner is welcomed as one home-born.

That said, what are some of the frequently cited objections that need to be addressed with regard to the entrance of the children of sojourners into the Christian schools?

What if the school community would not support the change without incremental steps?

The nature of renewal necessitates such incremental steps (also called growth and learning). This will be true until the Lord returns. My advice to you if you are in a position of influence in this matter: determine the next best obedient incremental step and take it. Courage is not the absence of fear but the belief that something else is more important than one's personal fears.

Sojourn space constitutes evangelism—a function of the church, not the school.

Evangelism is a function of the church whereby some are called and commissioned to leave their Christian community (native element) and bring the gospel to other places. An evangelist for Christ who follows God's call to destinations "afar" becomes a sojourner in an unfamiliar place where they have no inherited rights. In the New Testament evangelism is a function solely of the church (Matthew 28:16–20; Ephesians 2:13–14); it was typified in the Old Testament in, for example, the call and commission of Jonah to Nineveh.

Throughout the Old and New Testaments hosting sojourners (and others in need) is seen as a function of the entire covenant community, which shares both blessings and responsibilities with those who are drawn near. This can be done at church, home, school, work, or wherever a believer finds himself legitimately interacting with sojourners while living in a faith community. This concept was typified in the Old Testament by the realities of *ger* and *towshab* (see chapters 3 and 4) and realized in the New Testament when the "middle wall of partition was broken down" (verses 11–22).

Changes to Christian institutions have watered down their commitment and effectiveness, resulting in their becoming Christian in name only.

A scenario in which many have undergone change for the wrong reason(s) does not negate the possibility of change for a right reason. History is replete with examples of expedient rather than obedient reforms, and Christian organizations are not exempted from an obligation to reexamine their history and tradition just because they fear the results of ill-conceived reform. If an organization is unable or unwilling to consider renewal, the battle for Truth is largely lost, regardless of how well the doctrine has been formulated or the law outwardly kept. Again, I'm not claiming to have definitive answers, but I am offering a perspective on how the underlying heart problems might be addressed. In Christ, these problems could be faced with Grace and Truth rather than through a fear-induced felt need to control. I am suggesting that leaders in Christian education study the standard of scriptural sojourn, consider a renewed way of being Christ-like, and then take a consistent stand. Remaining neutral and/or inconsistent indicates that being Christian in name only is already an issue.

What if sojourners seek enrollment for the wrong reasons?

The "right reasons" for the enrollment of the children of sojourners into the Christian school, as we have seen, were invented by fear controls, not by obedience to biblically communicated pre-qualifiers for such admission. I have yet to meet a sojourner who desired admission based on a full understanding of God in Christ and of Christian education. Parenthetically, in twenty plus years I've met precious few *professed Christian parents* who could fully articulate a biblically formulated defense of Christian education.

It is the mandate of Christian educators to teach Christ in all content and process. But if the conceptions and understandings on the part of any applicant or attendee are treated as the foundation for change in terms of what is taught about Christ, it is the Christian school that has the problem. A spiritual problem. Fix *that* problem. God will do what God will do with faithful teaching. It is far less important what is understood by an enrollee (or their parents) upon entrance into the institution (except for content planning purposes) than what is understood by the same student or parent(s) when exiting the school.

Sojourners add messy problems . . .

Yes indeed. But I hope you'll allow me to interject here that there never was, and never will be, a shortage of sinners or messes in the Christian school. But God willing, there will always be teaching of Christ in content and process *to* the sinner and the addressing of the mess. A vigorous and myopic attempt to maintain outwardly clean cups poses a great danger to the Christian community because it ignores or distracts from *inner* mess-washing. When the inside of one's own cup receives regular cleaning, the fear of dealing with the inside or outside of another's cup (Matthew 23:26) is greatly ameliorated. The meticulous keeping of outwardly clean cups, then, is a far greater danger on the entire ecumenical landscape than the potential mess caused by the addition of sojourners.

Faithful Christ-followers will not draw back from the mess either of the children of believers or of the offspring of those from afar off. Refusal to draw back from the believers' mess is the most valuable teaching methodology used by the Master Teacher *because it takes away our fear of learning from Him* (1 John 4:18). Is that teaching methodology being well reflected? In the context of the fall, expectations of less or even of no mess are frankly silly. And fear of a mess while confessing Christ is sin: "His grace is sufficient . . . , and His strength is made perfect in weakness" (2 Corinthians 12:9).

Is this a very hard job, and does it demand a lot of resources?

Yes and yes. I have met several Christian school leaders who are fairly convinced that sojourner space is a command of Scripture but whose objections are related to how much work this would take in the context of scarce resources. I agree and continue, along with my colleagues, to work for and seek the needed resources. Hard work and a chronic need for additional resources are part and parcel of Christian service. The reality is, though, that where God's finger points His hand clears the path. God makes Himself responsible for all of the consequences into which our obedience leads. "How will we do this?" is not an appropriate question until "What is obedient?" in any given context has been answered. Steps taken in an obedient direction, *as God provides*, are faithful.

The presence of the children of sojourners will jeopardize the morality of and/or dilute the "Christian" population.

I agree that this will happen in the Christian school where Truth (Christ) is not taught and integrated unapologetically into every content area; is not preeminent in the consideration of all accountability; and is not held tightly as the "third strand" of Ecclesiastes 4:12, providing a standard for all relationships. My suggestion for renewal is predicated on the assumption that there are indeed leaders in Christian education who are committed to applying that Truth, with Grace, and that it is only their heads, hands, and hearts that are bound by various constructs of fear—whether internally or externally derived.

Christian communities deteriorate and dilute because they are spiritually weak, not because outside influences are stronger than Christ. Believing that spiritual weakness results from an influx of outside influences exposes a lack of understanding about sin's internal influence. Religious communities of all kinds could be kept morally clean and wholesome on the basis of pre- or post-qualifying to ensure that all potential members are a "fit." But Christian communities are spiritually healthy because they consistently teach Christ in a Christ-like way, while rejecting fear. In the context of Christian education, the notion that the sin outside the community is of greater concern than that within the community continues to grow steadily and is another example pointing to the need for spiritual renewal.

Christian schools will be at legal risk if they open admission to sojourners.

The reality is that Christian schools will be—and are—at legal risk, period. But they will be at the *least* legal risk with admissions policies and processes that clearly state faith-based and biblically supported beliefs while allowing enrollment to any *who by their own choice wish to enter mutually responsible association* within that gracious and unapologetic community. The choice to enroll is made by the one who has been candidly informed of the nonnegotiable teaching that will take place and of the mutually responsible association that will be entered into. There is no discrimination on the part of the school because the school doesn't do the choosing; the participant chooses when fully aware of the implications.

The greatest legal risk is in policies that prequalify or post-qualify (discriminate) in terms of who is or is not worthy of receiving Christ-centered instruction, based upon artificial measurements of religious "fitness" *that the school cannot consistently enforce.* (An aside: who among those enrolled by their own well-informed choice is not "fit" to receive instruction on Christ?) Christian schools don't express the issue, of course, in quite the way I've phrased it here, but consider whether or not there is often a clear objective to ensure, through the application of "fitness" criteria, that participants all resemble the presumed saved. Since salvation cannot be measured or timed, and since outward characteristics of salvation are highly irregular and inconsistent as believers grow in faith, the refusal to enroll or the willingness to expel on this contrived basis is easily identified in the courts as discrimination, making the institution highly vulnerable to legal consequence.

Legal risk for Christian communities in the 21st century has a lot to do with the way the wind blows; that's the nature of the perilous times in which we live (2 Thessalonians 2, 2 Timothy 3). In the words of the Old Testament leader Joshua, "Be strong and of good courage" (Joshua 1:9). *But this also has a lot to do with the failure of Christians to be consistently Christ-like.*

Allowing admission of the children of particular kinds of sinners is condoning particular sin(s).

I'm suggesting a singular objective for the Christian school: to teach Christ in content and process, primarily to the children of believers but also to those of sojourners who are drawn by God's design toward a desire to be taught. The building or breaking of the school-family relationship follows faithfulness to that teaching and consistent application of discipleship based upon what participants *do* within the school rather than on what they *think or believe* in the school setting. It is not the Christian school's mandate, as it is for the church, to exercise spiritual authority outside the school's bounds.

Not all sins are equivalent in terms of social impact and consequence, this is true. But the Christian school is not rightly engaged in social engineering. God's rule and purpose in individuals are realized primarily through faithful teaching and faithful preaching. Teaching Christ faithfully requires that sin be understood as it appears in the eyes of God, not in the eyes of human beings whose outer cups have been washed. The impact and consequence of all sin is equivalent in the eyes of God and when standing in the court of God (Genesis 6:5; 8:21; Psalm 51:5; Jeremiah 17:9; Ephesians 2:1–3).

The impetus for condoning or not condoning particular sins comes not from the Word or from our personal holiness. It is based primarily on our own aversion to particular sins (discrimination); avoidance of the pain and mess of sin (cowardliness); or our attempts to isolate "our own" children and families from the influence of "bad" people (selfishness and self-righteousness). Christians tend to label as sins those particular infractions of the law or negative behaviors they do not believe themselves to be guilty of. There are many instances in which non-negotiable truth and gracious consequence could be applied as an appropriate response to *any* kind of sin that is outwardly exhibited in the school, based on a legitimate desire to bring the power of Christ to bear on the devastating effects of sin. Bringing Truth motivated by discrimination, cowardliness, or self-righteousness, however, is *not* Christian love; it is diabolical.

Teaching Christ in content and process within the school entails a partnership of mutually agreed upon responsibilities for behavioral and academic guidelines, as outlined in a student-parent handbook. I do not find biblical justification for extending the moral or spiritual authority of a Christian school (as opposed to a Christian church) beyond those bounds in order to "police" the beliefs, thoughts, conscience, and/or lifestyle of involved participants *outside* the school community. A later chapter will deal with responses to the influences that (all) sinners will certainly bring *into* the school community.

The Christian school has appropriate oversight (biblically, socially, and legally) of the content and provisions of the student-parent handbook, of hiring, and of overall content and process. I grant that when the Christian school is faithful to that over which it has appropriate authority, this will necessitate some challenging conversations regarding every facet of the school's life and identity—but to avoid the difficult conversations by erecting artificial, fear-driven controls is not faithful; it is faith*less*.

The Christian school may (and should), wherever appropriate, discuss and teach what God says about sins, but to imagine a right or responsibility beyond the confines of spiritual (Church) or legal (State) authority is simply overreaching God's intended boundary. The Christian school is both responsible and able to teach Christ in content and process, which includes the teaching of the Law and all other content of the Old and New Testament. *So teach.* Relationships within the context of a gracious environment deepen quickly, opening many opportunities for meaningful conversations that will include truth without apology, wherever called for, to the children of believers or to those of parents coming from afar off.

Sojourners will outnumber professed Christians.

Sojourner space in graciously unapologetic Christian school communities will likely be self-limiting because Christ (the Word, *logos*) is self-limiting (John 1:5[1]; Hebrews 4:12).[2] According to God's design participants will either be drawn into fellowship with Christ (John 1:12–13)[3]; be repelled by the teaching of Christ (1:10[4]; 1 John 2:19)[5]; or live in comfortable compliance with that teaching and its behavioral ramifications (Matthew 22:11–14).[6] Relative to total population, Christ followers (as opposed to biblically religious people) will always be a small minority. Given a faithful and authentic reflection of Christ's way of being in grace and truth, the Christian school will *likely* be physically sustainable—but *certainly* the organization will be spiritually healthy.

Consider carefully the many times over the course of many years in which a prayer for revival has been heard in Christian schools, as well as in Christian churches and Christian families. What *if* the number of sojourners in a school or church grows large, and many are drawn near to the teaching of Christ in both content and process? If many are drawn near, and then *into* the promise of Christ, this is called a revival. A revival may or may not be God's will—I'm not in a position to say. What I *am* wondering is why believers would pray for a revival while objecting to an influx of people? Such a scenario would seem to be an obvious contradiction.

Conclusion

Controls rooted in fear lull biblical faith communities into blindness. The most dangerous enemies—the wayward hearts fearing to let go of controls rightly belonging to God—are not outwardly visible. The sojourner, unlearned in Scripture, *does* and *will* pervert Truth through ignorance, but isn't ignorance the very problem a Christian school is equipped to rectify? The greater danger is that those learned in Scripture, while they are redeemed but not yet fully restored, would pervert Truth through subtle craft. Whether or not fellow leaders agree with my conclusions is of far less concern to me than whether they will be satisfied to lead in environments of neutrality, inconsistency, or mediocrity. Listen to Paul's exhortation: "You believers: watch; stand firm in faith; act like men; be strong. Let everything you do be done in love; *the opposite of fear*" (1 Corinthians 16:13, 14, italics mine).

> "For if you thoroughly amend your ways and your doings; if you thoroughly execute judgment between a man and his neighbor; if you do not oppress the sojourner, the fatherless, and the widow, and shed not innocent blood in this place, neither walk after other gods to your hurt: then I will cause you to dwell in this place, in the land that I gave to your fathers, for ever and ever." (Jeremiah 7:5–7)

6

A Renewed Way to Be

"And the Word was made flesh and lived among us, (and we have seen His glory, the glory as of the only begotten of the Father), full of grace and truth." (John 1:14)

The Teeter-Totter

Exclusivity results in a particular way of being gracious. At this teeter-point, grace is limited to comfortable exchanges of care and applications of distant assistance. It does not risk or deliver excessively, particularly close to home. It does not cause the gracious one to be despised or rejected, filled with sorrow, or befriended by grief. Men do not hide their faces from this grace (Isaiah 53:3).[1] Around this kind of grace, truth is extolled and entombed (Matthew 23:27)[2] in (self-) righteous principles, (heroic) efforts, and (pure) religion.

The error of this grace originates with egocentric rather than with Christ-centered Truth. This particular variety of gracious one cites a defense of truth as justification for his stingy grace. He argues that too much grace would risk the truth, as though Truth would be rendered void were grace extended beyond the confines of his personal comfort and safety. He believes that God is glorified and approving when tears are shed from a safe distance and when self-defined truth is required *of others* as a prerequisite for the receipt of grace. This is precisely how one would reflect the Grace of Christ if this individual had earned it by his own adherence to Truth.

At the totter-point, grand objectives such as soul-winning, earth-restoring, and kingdom-building result in particular ways of being "in truth." Of necessity, the truth is defined by the experience and intellect of individuals working to meet their targeted ends. It promises much in the way of saving, restoring, and kingdom building but delivers little. This fluctuating truth makes men the princes of peace (Jeremiah 6:14)[3] based on their avoidance of meaningful conflict. Of this brand of "truth" Christ is not the stumbling stone (1 Peter 2:8).[4] Around this kind of "truth" grace flows indulgently, while Christ's purposes are renounced (Luke 14:26–27)[5] in favor of so-called kindness.

The error of this purported truth originates with egocentric rather than with Christ-centered grace. This variety of truth-teller champions grace by avoiding internal distress or conflict. He uses lavish grace as justification for impotent "truth." This champion of grace would rather the Truth return void (Isaiah 55:11)[6] than be held accountable for resolving the pain of its implications. With grace he acts as though the world needs saving from the naked truth. He believes that the kingdom will come through applications of grace without the necessity of divulging the inconvenient truth. This is exactly how one would reflect the truth if Christ had died so that men could avoid the knowledge of their conflict with God and produce the kingdom of God in *this* world (John 18:35–37)[7] through their own meritorious work.

Teeters and totters attempt to resolve the warfare between self and God on their own terms. All along the teeter-totter ride are nuances of truth without Grace and grace without Truth. Following copious stellar examples from the visible church, Christian schools have teetered and tottered along this dangerous path, reflecting an unbalanced and inconsistent Christ. Perhaps the answer to the problem for those who teach Christ is to follow the simple pattern of Christ's way of life among us: limitless Grace and unyielding Truth, standing firm on the glorious balance point of Christ alone (1:14).

A Way of Life

If John 1:14 were paraphrased in a manner sounding as though we believed it had contemporary application to our way of life, it might sound like this: "'Christ continues to live through believers on the earth, (and the glory of God in Christ can be seen through them), because they are living in and then reflecting the fullness of His grace and truth." This *is* applicable, of course—the "believers living in and reflecting the fullness of His grace and truth," I mean.

A believer is not someone who has pre-qualified, professed, or been pronounced "saved" by the constructs of human beings. A believer is the undeserving recipient (Romans 3:9–10)[8] of Grace (Ephesians 2:8–9)[9] and Truth (John 17:17),[10] perfectly and completely balanced upon the righteousness and sacrifice of Christ. The believer brings nothing to the acquisition of salvation. The bearing of fruit is a *result* of salvation, not a *cause*.

I've already pointed out that fears have led to easy grace and safe truth and away from a full reflection of biblical covenant balanced upon the righteousness and sacrifice of Christ alone. There is far less good news in an unbalanced gospel. Mature believers find it insipid (thus often fleeing Christian schools), while "those afar off, as many as the Lord shall call" find it soon unsatisfying (thereby frequently coming and going).

For an organization to reflect a Christ-like way of being, it must do more than teach what Christ taught and deal reactively with concerns as they come up. It must teach what He taught while reflecting His balanced way of being in Grace and Truth, all the while moving proactively toward Him in love. Notice an example of Jesus' "way of being" in Luke 15:1–3: "Then publicans and sinners *drew near* to hear Jesus. But the Pharisees and scribes *murmured*, saying, This man *gives sinners access* to Himself, and He eats with them. Then Christ *taught them* with this parable, saying . . ." (paraphrase mine).

Many and various sinners drew near and were given access to Jesus. They did not feel sufficiently alienated to prevent such overtures. This speaks to us of His Grace. In the course of welcoming access, Jesus taught the religious and the non-religious alike, the sinners and the self-righteous, without apology. This speaks to us of His Truth. After the teaching people either drew nearer, were repelled, or continued in compliant company. Two simple questions:

is Jesus' grace reflected today in a way that causes some religious and non-religious sinners of all varieties to feel drawn to approach the Christian school? And is Jesus' truth taught in a way that draws some nearer, repels others, and allows still others to continue in compliant company?

Religious zealots felt threatened by the approach of sinners and murmured. And oh, how the murmurs are heard today. "I pay thousands to protect my children from . . ."; "My children are spiritual, those influences will . . ."; "I would—really, I want to—but I have principles . . ."; "I want to be gracious, but there's a limit, right?" And of course: "Our tradition . . ." Another simple question: are admissions pre-qualifiers or rigid, punitive structures of discipline the result of zealous murmurs that have "won out" and successfully created constructs that prohibit the approach and/or access of, not to mention the bother of dealing with sinners in Grace and Truth?

In the hearing of all who had drawn near, Jesus taught. Christian schools would find the spiritual strength to teach Christ, reflecting the fullness of His Grace and Truth, if sacrifices of copious time, energy, and cogitation were not given to self-assigned responsibilities such as protecting the kingdom and saving souls. Simply teach Christ with authority. Everything else that God intends will follow from obedience. Jesus taught all who drew near without the personal anger, defensiveness, discrimination, insecurity, prejudgment or arrogance that result from fear. And in the power of His might (Ephesians 6:10)[11] the Christian school may do so as well—as soon as "letting go of fear" commences.

This is the way of being that could dominate the landscape of Christian education: a group of grace-filled believers training their children (Acts 2:39a) and attracting those "afar off, as many as the Lord shall call" to draw near (v. 39b) without fear. Further, this group of believing leaders could be full of truth: teaching Christ in content and process, rightly dividing the Word of Truth, and casting down every imagination that raises itself against the knowledge of God and of obedience to Christ (2 Corinthians 10:3–5). Some families would draw closer, others would be repelled, and still others would continue in comfortable compliance, just as it has been throughout His-story and will continue be until the Lord returns to conclude that story.

Many claim Grace and appear undisciplined, permissive, lenient, and overly adaptable. Many claim Truth and appear disciplined, rigid, exacting, and maladaptive. Few seek a balance in Grace and Truth (claiming competence at neither)—while clinging to Christ's strength, which is made perfect in weakness. Unbalanced toward Truth, the Father is reflected without the Son. Unbalanced toward Grace, the Son is reflected without the Father. Balance in Grace and Truth reflects the will of the Father, the work of the Son, and the indwelling of the Holy Spirit all at the same time. Believers have been reborn not to a spirit of fear to continue a slavish run from the old master, but to the balance of love in a free, unbounded race toward the new One.

Is what I'm suggesting difficult? Yes. It requires leaders in Christian education who believe that Christ is all to let go of fear (all the time) and lead by measuring *self* against the standard of Christ's righteousness. The more common measurement is a personal, traditional, or community self-righteousness that is demanded of *others* because the *self* has managed to keep that misdefined righteousness well enough to soothe his or her fears for a time. It's a log and eye kind of situation (Matthew 7:1–4).[12] "Come unto me, all you that are heavy laden with sins . . . " (11:28a).

And no, because the righteousness that results from His Truth completes what we have left undone (Philippians 3:9),[13] and the sacrifice that results from His Grace satisfies the demand of a law we cannot keep (Matthew 22:36–40).[14] ". . . and I will give you rest" (11:28b). Is it impossible? Yes, for the self it is. But with God it is absolutely possible (19:26).[15] It is pleasant (and quite popular) to quote that "there is therefore now no condemnation . . ." (Romans 1:8), but it is far superior to live in the liberty of believing this amazing news.

Christ taught indiscriminately in Word and deed among those who drew near. He did not refuse fishes and loaves to particular sinners (Matthew 14:13–21; Mark 6:30–44; Luke 9:10–17; John 6:1–15), nor did He discriminate when healing lepers, though in the story Jesus tells only one returned to offer gratitude (Luke 17:11–19). That errant woman at the well was not refused water prior to getting her life straightened out (John 4:5–42). Christ taught truth and *is* Truth, while maintaining Grace that attracted many from far to near and from that near vantage point *into* His sacrifice and righteousness.

It is obviously impossible to live fully without fear and thereby be fully gracious and truthful. But to live with the devoted intention of replacing motivations of fear with motivations of love, so that Christ will be reflected in His Grace and Truth, is obedient and also highly instructive to those we teach. This lifestyle makes for a graciously unapologetic environment that is spiritually growing and vibrant. It attracts some potential enrollees and repels others. Regardless of the outcome for an organization or for any individual—after all which is God's business—*obedience means sacrificing the need to control the outcome.*

> "But I say to you, love those who oppose the Truth. . . . so that you may be the children of your Father who is in heaven: because He makes the sun to rise on the evil and the righteous in Christ alone, and sends rain on the justified in Christ alone and the unjustified. What good is it if you serve only those that are in agreement with Truth; even the publicans love their friends." (Matthew 5:44–45, paraphrase mine)

7

Fuzzy-Buzz Words Defined

"By wisdom a house is built, and by understanding it is established; and by knowledge the rooms are filled with all precious and pleasant riches." (Proverbs 24:3–4, NASB)

Fear is at the top of a slippery slope: it threatens, control ensues, love retreats, confusion reigns, dissent appears, *and well-defined words are subsequently defined by fuzzy emotion.* Grace and truth become ambiguous buzzwords to make nice and easy peace. The slippery slope continues in a vicious cycle of "what to do" crisis and response initiatives designed to sooth apprehension about losing self-assigned battles engaged on behalf of God. The cycle ends where fear of the Lord begins. For relief, this fear (Proverbs 9:10–12)[1] requires well-defined words.

Let's consider for a moment how life would be lived by one who believed that grace could relieve people's fears, both of God and of all lesser things (Romans 8:1),[2] if truth could elevate humans to eternal fellowship with God (John 8:31–32),[3] and if divine power could make all of this possible (Matthew 19:24–26).[4] If these realities were believed to be true through Christ, the words *grace* and *truth* would require careful definition (2 Timothy 2:15)[5] and then clear reflection (John 13:13–17[6]; 1 John 2:6[7]) as fears were dissolved in trust in God (Proverbs 3:5–6).[8] Some definition is attempted in this chapter because these statements *are* in fact true, but the slippery slope of fear has resulted in widespread fuzzy-buzz. While these truths are often confessed, they are not always well defined or clearly reflected. The words themselves, in terms of their definitions, require renewal.

Christ is the meaning and objective on which every realm of life rests and in whom all learning is rooted. Consider a scenario in which the full revelation of Jesus Christ is integrated into all learning *and* a Christ-like way of being in grace and truth (John 1:14) is consistently reflected and passionately pursued in every organizational and relational application. Initiating and maintaining such a scenario would require words that are well defined. But also, and more importantly, it would require that the fear of God and of lesser things be progressively sacrificed on the altar of devotion to Christ alone.

Grace, Truth, and Other Definitions

Grace and truth are divine qualities we'd rather not clearly define because doing so leads to an insufferable reality: ***sin** is corruption of the whole being, leaving people spiritually dead and therefore unable to respond to God.* This corruption is manifested as both passive and active aggression against God. Passively, sinners fail to live a righteous life (don't do as they're told). Actively, they succeed at living wickedly (do what they're told not to). Motivating this aggression is a heart that does not love God or neighbor in any way, a heart in which only self-love influences action. Sinners are spiritually dead, possessing neither grace nor truth. Each fallen image-bearer (sinner) lives under a death sentence, having no expectation other than eternal and complete separation from God—a condition called hell.

God designs and executes a plan to bring some sinners to enjoy the intimate friendship with Himself that ultimately excels the relationship that Adam enjoyed in Eden—in Christ, full of grace and truth, that relationship is rendered imperishable. As a new creation in Christ, the believer begins a journey *toward* the completion of the incorruptible life Christ has earned, rather than running *away from* the fears that lie behind. Because of this, *the **deepest need** and **highest good** of fallen creatures is intimate, personal, relational union with the sacrifice (in payment for active aggression) and the righteousness* *(substitute for passive aggression) of Jesus Christ.* All other needs are subordinate. All other goods are inferior.

Pause for a moment to take in the implications of the godhead dwelling in flesh. The qualities of grace and truth are implanted and continue to grow as organic beings experience new life as recipients of Christ. Christ incarnate lived the *way* of grace, and the *truth* of the godhead, and now reigns in the resurrected *life* he earned for those He saves (John 14:6).[9] The plan requires the will of the Father and the application of the Spirit. But for success, this plan requires *fullness* of grace and truth from Christ.

Grace *is an unmerited attitude of favor* (Ephesians 2:8–9)[10] *motivated exclusively by the pleasure of God* (1:5–6),[11] *and unbroken by any remaining corruption* (2:5) *in the object of favor.* God continues to maintain this attitude (Philippians 1:6)[12] until mortality and corruption put on immortality and incorruptibility (1 Corinthians 15:53).[13] Grace is the attitude, and sacrifice the resulting action by which Christ meets one's deepest need. It was His sacrifice, by grace, that appeased the wrath of God against sinners (1 John 4:10).[14] Many other grace-related topics become fruitful for teaching Christ *after* a believer has become cognizant of the divine favor that has been directed toward the self and reflects a corresponding attitude *toward* his fellow human beings. The recipient at this point is called to be a reflector.

Truth *is the eternal, unyielding, singular standard of "right-ness" by which fellowship with God is attained.* Jesus Christ *is* truth; He possesses and presents the fullness of divinity in His flesh. As fully man He lives in complete righteousness and is Himself the unbending standard of measure. God cannot and will not befriend corrupted image-bearers. Truth is the standard, and righteousness the resulting action by which Christ delivers the highest good. It is this righteousness, in truth, that earns the friendship of God toward sinners (Philippians 3:9–11).[15]

Again, many other truth-related topics become fruitful for teaching Christ *after* a person becomes cognizant of Christ's righteousness fully substituting for their own corruption. Even the fruit of righteousness that follows belief is no better than "filthy rags" in the sight of God (Isaiah 64:6a)[16] and also requires completion through Christ's righteousness. In this way believers are rendered holy in God's eyes, just as God is holy (1 Peter 1:13–16).[17] Such an individual lives with an attitude of favor toward others, while seeking personal righteousness reflective of Christ *toward* both God and his fellow humans. Once again, the recipient is called to be a reflector.

With grace and truth, God in Christ conjoins two diametrically opposed realities: a favorable disposition toward sin-marred beings (grace) and the purity of His divine character (truth). When joined, these qualities are sufficient to address the deepest need and highest good of every image-bearing creature. Believers progressively reflect the resolution of these opposing realities through *personal* sacrifice and righteousness to reflect Christ meeting their own *personal* deepest need and highest good. A believer reflects Christ to all their neighbors while standing in the very presence of God, having received from Him the gift of Christ. Further, a Christ-like reflection does not permit the individual any motivations of personal gain from the exchange with neighbors beyond the joy of obedience to God (Hebrews 10:7).[18] This way of being projects a glorious array of glimpses into the person and character of Jesus Christ on behalf of sinners.

Many spiritual fruits adorn the organizational tree where Christ Himself is the standard of measurement for grace and truth. Christ is the firstfruits of a harvest that flows freely through yielded vessels when barriers of passive and aggressive resistance are being broken down. These barriers come down when fears of God and of lesser things have been relieved. In such an organization biblical content is integrated into all learning and Christ's way of being can be glimpsed in acts and interactions throughout each day, in all relationships and spanning the vast spectrum of possible circumstances.

This is learning in the brilliant light of Christ: balanced reflections of grace and truth in all content and process, where the learner's value and the educator's significance are not dependent on any particular outcome or exchange between the two. All other learning environments are variations of the shadows in Plato's cave.[19]

Schools run well by moral people, as well as by hypocrites and the self-righteous, are able to mimic many principles of Scripture. But none can successfully fake the fruit of repentance and restoration, as failure to "measure up" regularly interrupts a pervasive way of being Christ-like, where "His strength is made perfect in our weakness" (2 Corinthians 12:9).

Suppose a school calling itself Christian were to teach all of the requisite content about Christ and also high-quality content in all the appropriate academic disciplines. Suppose that management were to successfully and consistently maintain outward morality within this school. And finally, suppose that only best practices *du jour* were engaged in teaching and learning. This very good, or even great school would still have no capacity to reflect grace (a favorable disposition toward *corrupted* beings) or truth (the measure of *Christ's* character). Participants could be kind to each other and call it grace, and they could be well behaved and call it truth. Leadership, admittance, and/or continued attendance could be earned on the basis of outward works. Why teach Christ at all in an environment where diametrically opposed realities (favorable disposition toward sin-marred beings and friendship with God) can be resolved without Christ (Mark 2:17)?[20] It may be that public and other non-public schools are actually preferable alternatives to the Christian school I've just described: the wolf in a public school is at least not clothed as a sheep (Matthew 7:15).[21]

Keep in mind that the imaginary school I've just described is doing all the "right stuff." So what? That alone does not make it Christian. In a school that is rightly called Christian Christ is reflected in believers whose doing flows from a heart restored by the favorable disposition and divine character of Christ. They are *recipients*, growing in motivation and proactivity toward Him *as reflectors*, having been sacrificed on the altar of devotion to Him and thus rejecting fears of God and lesser things. No doubt there will be a lot of "doing stuff" in a graciously unapologetic Christian school, but infinitely more important is that the doing will flow from hearts pervaded by a Christ-like way of being.

8

A Secret-Place Conversation

"Only let your conversation be as it is fitting the good news of Christ." (Philippians 1:27a, paraphrase mine)

The secret place of the Most High is in His shelter (Psalm 91:1),[1] where those who fear Him (25:14)[2] have been relieved (Romans 8:1)[3] in the grace and truth of Jesus Christ and find that restored friendship with God is unbreakable (verses 35–39).[4] A conversation springs to life in that secret place, where the old self and the new creature in Christ (Colossians 3:9–10)[5] have persistent inner dialogue that flows into a life-dominating conversation.

This infectious conversation begins with the soul at rest in Christ *alone*, where fears of God and of lesser things are being daily relieved. The new self speaks grace and truth to the old self, whose remaining corruption, infirmity, and fear continually seek dominance (Romans 7:18–24).[6] The new self loves God more and more, and in the process learns to love the self rightly. Secret-place conversations are a way of life leading *toward* the full measure of Christ (Ephesians 4:13).[7]

That full measure of Christ is being pursued when one is able to *yield* one's rights in order to sacrifice on behalf of others (grace) and to *wield* God's whole law in righteousness (truth), while trusting and obeying God's plan and directive. In doing these things Christ was without *personal* limitation within the *boundaries* of the godhead. Like the frog immersed in water that is slowly increasing in temperature, Christian educators have grown comfortable swimming in self-assigned boundaries of grace in order to justify personal limits in truth. Notable examples are restrictive admissions policies and/or punitive focus on the outward acts of others, as opposed to the inward cleansing of the self.

When Christian school leaders *lead* from the strength of secret-place conversations, this engages others in the spiritual dialogue of redemption, and the culture of the organization is renewed in a Christ-like way of being. All measures of "rightness" other than Christ's way of being allow fears to drive group norms that dictate methods of achievement ending in mediocrity or in a bastardized form of excellence sired by the will of a different father (John 8:44–45).[8]

God "relents from sending calamity" when His people return to Him with their whole heart. Intense *heart* scrutiny dominates wherever Christ is believed to be all. "The LORD declares that even now you must return to me with your whole heart, with fasting and weeping and mourning. Rip your hearts apart, not your garments. Return . . ." (Joel 2:12, paraphrase mine). It is time, as it were, to "grow up" and blow the trumpet (1:1) in Zion, to "sound the alarm in God's holy mountain." If Christian education is in trouble, it is not because Christ has abandoned his people but because His people have left the standard of Christ *alone*.

To lead with Christ *alone* (as opposed to sprinkling Him like pixie dust over self-determined ends or self-righteous norms) produces abundant spiritual fruit, from which all the fruits of excellence flow. Academic excellence (biblically defined) and the wise use of temporal strategies *follows* when a Christ-like way of being *leads*. However, *Christ* will not *follow* academic excellence where temporal strategies *lead* (Ecclesiastes 2:11)[9] or where self-reliance and self-righteousness are featured more prominently than the mandate to "trust and obey."

Relentless inner dialogue that measures the self by the impossible standard of Christ, all the while resting in His sacrifice and reaching for His righteousness, will be foolishness (1 Corinthians 3:19–21)[10] and a stumbling stone (1 Peter 2:7–8)[11] to some. But others will discover through such conversation a panoramic vista of deeper learning that is immeasurably augmented in all areas, because greater and lesser fears (barriers to learning) are being daily relieved. When viewed as more than a personal and social-utilitarian acquisition of knowledge, education driven by inner conversations toward a Christ-like way excels all other forms and applications of instruction.

As an aside, allow me to clarify that I do use dashboard indicators and that I am well read, data driven, and qualified and that I understand the challenges of a rapidly changing world. I point this out because "too spiritual" is the dismissive label all too frequently applied to my suggestions. "Too temporal" is the counter-reply of this book. Results of the fall and curse were, are, and always will be limiting factors in teaching and learning. This necessitates the use of data, metrics, and other temporal strategies in every educational (or other) setting. I merely suggest that temporal measures be discussed and vigorously applied only after a "Christ *alone*" measure is renewed in the hearts of persons holding titles designating them as spiritual and Christ-centered leaders.

A spiritual foundation established in secret-place conversations results in freedom to *yield* and *wield*, to *trust* and *obey*, without fear. For instance, imagine that a secret-place dialogue would lead board members to *yield* a sense of safety that has been falsely perceived and to *wield* admissions conversations in non-negotiable truth, to *obey* the command of God about the children of sojourners while *trusting* God for the outcome. Secret-place conversations flow outwardly in living examples of renewal (or *re*-formation, if you prefer), leading the community in a Christ-like way.

Even though secret-place conversations always produce results that are in some way flawed, freedom to learn from humanly flawed results flourishes when fear of condemnation is relieved. Continuous re-calibration toward a clearer reflection of Christ leads to progressively clearer understandings of everything else that may be studied, and is consistent with the gifting of God in the learner. Engaging in this life-dominating conversation on exactly what to yield and wield, on how to trust and obey in any given context, is indeed to stand fast in one spirit and to strive unafraid for the faith of the gospel (Philippians 1:27–28),[12] all the while refusing to hide or place blame (Genesis

3:8[13] and 12).[14] This is a conversational way of life that definitely fits with the good news of Christ.

In His flesh Christ's greatest temptations were to yield less than complete trust to God's will for Himself as the sacrificial substitute and to wield God's law in less than complete obedience as imputed righteousness. Christ's sacrifice pays the debt for active sin (doing as told not to); His righteousness is substituted for passive sin (not doing as told). Salvation is dependent on the fullness of both. *Christ was passive and trusting in sacrifice because of Grace and active and obedient in righteousness because of Truth.* In organizations that name Christ, however, active energy is more often expended to limit self-sacrifice and to project self-righteousness. The labels of trust and obedience are often falsely attributed to works that serve self-assigned objectives designed to "help" God resolve the tension between such diametrically opposed ideas as inner corruption and friendship with God. This tension, of course, can only be resolved in Christ *alone*.

Christian educators do face many ominous indicators, but the real and present danger is that of failing to trust God by allowing the old self to react to lesser fears or failing to obey God by seeking less than the full measure of Christ. A reactive way of being is rooted in the (unrealized or unaddressed) fear that God's way of trust and obey cannot possibly be effective, inviting the substitution of self-assigned objectives. But these objectives are "our" way instead of Christ's way—which is by biblical definition the *only* way. Our Lord states unequivocally in John 6:38, "For I have come down from heaven not to do my will but to do the will of Him who sent me." Without intentionally pursuing the *way* of Christ, a human-centered way always dominates. Isaiah 53:6 puts it like this: "All we like sheep, have gone astray, each of us has turned to our own way."

A Christ-reflecting way is one of limitless grace and unyielding truth; of trusting and obeying within God's boundaries, amid the internal and external forces of evil perpetuated by the fall; and while rejecting fear. *Yikes!* Obviously, this secret-place conversation will not produce heaven on earth, "save" anyone in particular, or "build the kingdom." However, a Christ-like way of being is obedient and should dominate (1 John 2:6)[15] any organization claiming Christ as its Head. "God has chosen a thing considered weak in this world to confound the things considered strong in this world" (1 Corinthians 1:27, paraphrase mine). The way of Christ *is* the topmost *weak thing* in the opinion of this world.

A Christ-like way accomplishes "abundantly beyond all that we ask or think, according to the power that works within us" (Ephesians 3:20).[16] Organizational sustainability may or may not result from following His way, but neither is organizational sustainability (though it is an appropriate desire) the principal objective for leaders of Christ-centered organizations: what *is*, is to reflect the way of *obedience* while *trusting* that God has accomplished all things in Jesus Christ. God's plan for a particular organization might include extinction, sustainability, or anything in between. In every situation, God's *way* is for the obedience of Christ in grace and truth (2 Corinthians 10:5)[17] to engage the whole heart, regardless of how scary the actual or perceived outcomes may appear.

I do not consider it an exaggeration to claim that human-centered *ways* have contributed significantly to the development of Christian education in its current North American iteration—as well as to its current plight. These *ways* have been driven by fear and fear's resulting cowardice has served only to shrink the bounds of covenant and community life in ways that reflect the limits of our personal fears and that produce a will and a law intended to self-reflect the righteousness we imagine ourselves to have earned. It is painful for us to "own" the spiritual cowardice that has driven both our personal and our organizational limits. It is while engaged in this secret-place conversation that I most poignantly recognize myself to be guilty on both counts (1 Timothy 1:15).[18] And it is in the process of embracing the pain of this recognition that I find myself most able, on a daily basis, to lay hold of the renewable and reformative result: incredible deeper learning.

The fallen tree will be renewed *at the root* of Christ, and Christ alone. All of us (throughout His-story) have opted for the paths of Christ *and*—of Christ, that is, *along with* or *in addition to* whatever our first choice may be—in favor of what we perceive to be the higher-risk way of Christ *only*. It is only following our sincere repentance for that fundamental error that Christian education will move forward unimpeded on a path of spiritual renewal. The frenzied angst surrounding our hand-wringing discussions of "what to do" in order to "save" the nest ignores the reality that the nestlings cannot rest, or learn to fly, from *any* nest built in a tree whose trunk is fallen very near the ground, and whose roots are rotting. Christ *alone* stands ready to restore the root and nourish the tree; the fruit of the promise follows obedience to the command.

Will leaders in Christian education trust God by including sojourners in order to teach Christ in a *fully* covenantal community? And further, will they obey the law *toward God* with Christ as a personal standard of measure, rather than by engineering a religious facade to apply a self-attained standard of law to others? If they do, a spiritually renewed and structurally completed model of covenantal Christian schooling will emerge, incorporating meaningful space for sojourners while leaving little doubt that Christian educators are *only and all about* teaching Christ alone in all educational content and as a reflection of His way of being.

I urge Christian school leaders to reject limits and boundaries that have been erected on the basis of fear and to embrace instead the limitless freedom in Christ within the boundaries of God's will and law. Admittedly, this takes spiritual courage, but God's people will "be made willing in the day of His power" (Psalm 110:3) to yield or wield whatever God requires of them along that trust-filled and obedient way. To live the way of Christ in this darkening world is indeed to march in a triumphal procession, spreading everywhere the fragrance of the knowledge of Him (2 Corinthians 2:14).[19] Again, courage is not the absence of fear but the belief that obedience is more important than traditional, denominational, cultural, personal, or any other fears.

At this point in history artificial constructs in Christian education are not evidence of zealous spiritual life; they simply self-justify works of miserly grace and diminished truth. Returning to Christ *alone* will bring about rich cognitive dissonance, as fears are identified and relieved in secret-place conversations that flow into "all the issues of [school] life" (Proverbs 4:23). Looming spiritual calamities *will* resolve where tension-filled conversations *lead* toward the obedience of Christ. A reflection of Christ in limitless grace and truth, while trusting and obeying God's boundaries, is more than enough to heal and strengthen a fully covenantal community that has been broken by fears of lesser things than God. This is Truth, whether or not schools naming Christ are sustained organizationally.

> "I sought the Lord, and He heard me, and delivered me from all my fears" (from *fears*, not from circumstances or dangers, real or perceived). (Psalm 34:4, NKJV)

9

The Balance of Love

"This is the same way our love is made perfect, so that we may be bold in the Day of Judgment: *because as Jesus Christ is, so are we in the world.* There is no fear in love; but perfect (complete) love casts fear out because fear has torment. He that fears is not made complete in love." (1 John 4:17–18, paraphrase mine).

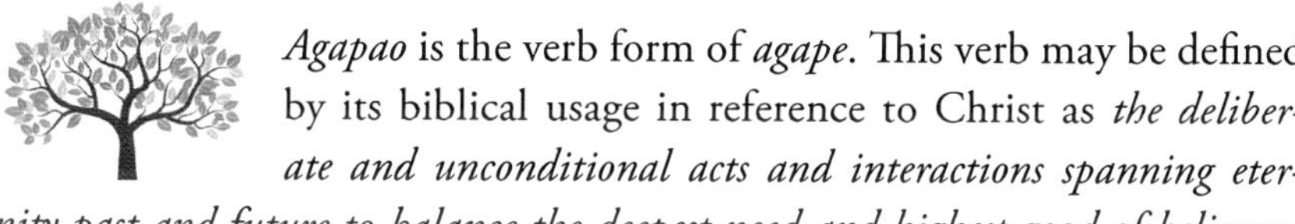

Agapao is the verb form of *agape*. This verb may be defined by its biblical usage in reference to Christ as *the deliberate and unconditional acts and interactions spanning eternity past and future to balance the deepest need and highest good of believers, the objective being that redeemed ones would glorify and enjoy Him forever, beginning in the now.* The English reduction of that *verb*iage to the noun-like word "love" is problematic for recipients of *agapao* who are seeking to reflect Christ. A more apt English rendering of *agapao* is "love toward."

Agapao balances grace and truth because it is the fulcrum upon which deliberate and unconditional (as opposed to reactive and emotive) movement advances toward the redemptive objective of the godhead. Christ's love directed *toward* the godhead is evidenced by "trust(ing) and obey(ing)" and by "yielding and wielding." That love results in deliberate and unconditional movement toward the redemptive purposes of the godhead. *Reflected* love is evidenced by the same kind of movement advanced in the direction of God's redemptive objective on behalf of the individual believer; first toward the complete measure of Christ (3:2)[1] and then by a reflection of Him in one's dealings *toward* all others (John 15:12).[2]

Every "jot and tittle" of the law having already been fulfilled in Christ, God's law for the believer is simply this: "*Agapao (or love toward) the Lord your God* with all your heart and with all your soul and with all your mind (trust and obey). This is the first and greatest commandment. And the second is like it: *Agapao (or love toward) your neighbor as yourself* (yield in grace and wield the truth). All the Law and the Prophets hang on these two commandments" (Matthew 22:37–40, paraphrase mine). In other words, be a deliberate and unconditional "copycat" reflection of Christ in love toward God and others, serving the glorification of Christ in His redemptive objective.

A graciously unapologetic community is neither antinomian nor legalistic; both are examples of reactive and emotive dominators of the flesh (Romans 6:1–2).[3] The balance of love is evidenced in environments that exhibit more deliberate concern about personal holiness and *less about pronouncing judgment on others*; more unconditional yielding of self and the wielding of truth, along with *less conditional self-protection and control of others*; and more deliberate and unconditional reflection of Christ in one's personal walk—along with *less talk, talk, talk*. Love that is *agapao* examines the *self* by the standard of Christ, which leads *toward* deliberate and unconditional acts and interactions of grace and truth, balanced by love, toward others.

I believe the biblically religious community has grown more satisfied with a "react and emote" modus operandi *toward others* when facing challenges that lie outside the preconditions set by the sensitivities of the group norm. The standard of Christ in self-reflection should cause a "react and emote" response toward the *self* because His standard brings to light constant challenges to the *reflector* of Christ and therefore progressively and repeatedly removes the log(s) in the reflector's eye. When seeing more clearly, the reflector is able to choose deliberately and unconditionally to reflect grace and truth wisely to the neighbor's speckled eye (Matthew 7:5).[4]

Reflectors of Christ determine what to do, or not to do, in secret-place conversations with the objective of providing glimpses of redemption in Christ through personal holiness (as opposed to self-righteousness) with a gracious disposition (as opposed to a focus on self-protection). As a result Christ is reflected in all interactions as the singular solution to the original and ultimate problem of all humankind: separation of the fallen creature from the Creator. The unseen God is *seen* at work in corrupted flesh as redeemed beings act with right-ness (or take responsibility for personal wrong-ness), regardless of what others do. In this way the upturned basket is continually lifted off the lamp (Luke 11:33),[5] and the Light is permitted with less and less inhibition to shine, oh, so brightly!

The deliberate and unconditional action in *agapao* necessitates regular and systematic crucifixion of self-determined ends (Galatians 2:20)[6] and self-righteous measures (5:24–25)[7] in favor of intentionally modeling the sacrifice and righteousness of Christ. Love toward others reflects a relationship with Christ as the deepest need and the highest good of all humanity. Inner tension over the sin of the self regularly results from secret-place conversations, and to resolve these tensions *first* within the self is to allow the self and its will to decrease while Christ increases (John 3:30).[8] It is the task of believing educators to interact in this way (that it, to decrease) because this is *Christ's way toward* or in the direction of—the believer. He is the Master Teacher, making Himself of no reputation (Philippians 2:6–7).[9]

Teeter-totter extremes of grace and truth are enervated by inner forces of the self rather than by the love of God and the neighbor. In religious circles these other forces produce expressions of self-reflecting spirituality resembling the relationship between Echo and Narcissus,[10] where Christ (or other gods) play the part of worshipful Echo and religious people that of self-adoring Narcissus. Self-reflecting religion in a biblically derivative community has produced traditionalists and denominationalists, but it has not reflected Christ *alone.* God draws an ominous plumb line (Amos 7:7–9)[11] wherever self-absorbed, biblically religious people are gazing at their own reflections.

Truth is most Christ-like where there is most concern about personal holiness when measured by the standard of Christ. This concern is a result of loving God. The sin of others is addressed by teaching Christ (wielding truth) within a relationship built on the favor shown to the self by Christ (yielding in grace).

Grace is Christ-like where no personal barriers are erected to the approach of "neighbors" (obey), even when all possible (and seemingly dangerous) corruptions remain intact in those who desire to approach the believer (trust). The exercise of such grace can only be the result of loving the neighbor. As mentioned earlier, relationships deepen (or repel) progressively where grace is prevalent, providing rich opportunities to speak the truth in love.

The fear of teaching Christ in an admissions scenario without religious preconditions is cast out when the neighbor is loved just as Christ has loved toward the self. Intimate personal union with Christ deepens as fears are relieved in grace and truth, instilling recognition of the immeasurable depth of Christ's balanced love, causing continual growth in a Christ-like way toward neighbors. On the other hand, various means of control (as opposed to order) expose the presence of dominating fears operating within Christian education. Grace and truth balanced by love toward God are themselves the ordained "controls" of the Spirit in the direction of His intended outcomes. Fear of lesser things than God drives a felt need to do more—or less—than commanded by the law of love.

Teachers of Christ are quick to assert that "love never fails" (1 Corinthians 13:8). Many students will wonder, though, why the love of Christ of which they speak fails to relieve educators (or parents) of fears that drive a felt need for control. Other students might be satisfied to mimic self-reflecting religiosity in the toxic soil of hypocrisy or self-righteousness, while still others will be labeled "good" and "Christian" by educators who talk about grace as though it can be earned and truth as though it lives by recitation. To declare that "love never fails" has great power when followed up by lives that shout "we will not fear" (Psalm 46), as reinforced by their stillness (a response that is neither emotive nor reactive) in the face of raging fears.

Allow me to ask and then to answer an essential question. What is the most integrative biblical way to teach? The most integrative biblical way to teach is *as a fallen image-bearer, rejecting fear out of love toward God (trust and obedience to the law of love), while reflecting the love of Christ in deliberate and unconditional acts and interactions of gracious sacrifice and righteous truth toward others, regardless of the outcome for self.* In other words, love as though you have never been, or will never be, hurt. This is the *most* integrative way to teach the mathematical distributive property, the days of creation, or any other subject matter at all. There are other important integration strategies, of course, but this one in particular brings "walk" to the talk.

Colleagues had earlier on urged me to consider the possibility that the Christ-like approach I'm seeking to describe would exert a negative impact on the faith, spirituality, and morality of the children of believers, primarily because the *way* I am advocating incorporates sojourners. The impact in the particular school in which I lead has put these fears to rest, at least for me. An authentic reflection of Christ has in fact been progressively augmented in this context because both board and staff leadership in this environment requires *yielding* the hypocrisy of fear-driven constructs and replacing them progressively with secret-place conversations that allow for love *toward* God while trusting and obeying. This internal conversation has flowed outward for the board, myself, and the staff in the direction of loving *toward* all covenant and sojourning families through teaching and learning with an eye toward *wielding* the truth (Christ) without apology in all school related contexts. Based on this experience I am confident in my assertion that communities are spiritually enhanced, not diminished, through clarified reflections of Christ's *lived* way, regardless of whether or not sojourners are intentionally allowed enrollment.

Graciously unapologetic educators *yield* fear and control in order to *wield* truth in a progressively more skillful way; *trusting* the Spirit of God to do the work He intends and *obeying* the law of focusing love in the direction of both God and then the neighbor. In spite of residual corruption, the believing educator rests in the knowledge that Christ moves with increased power through vessels that are progressively being emptied of self (2 Corinthians 12:9).[12] Perhaps the fear that is most difficult to talk about—indeed, that underlies the dysfunction in Christian education—is that *what God intends* might be in conflict with an educator's desired outcome related to the students' receipt of faith (or not). A clear reflection of Christ glorifies God and will be used by God, though not always to attract. Sometimes it repels.

This elemental and understandable fear must be overridden in a journey of love in the direction of fullness of friendship with God. First as a sojourner in "Adam," then as a citizen of heaven, and finally in seeking love toward the fullness of Christ, the self should not consider heavenly citizenship "a thing to be grasped" (Philippians 2:6–8).[13] Reflecting Christ while redeemed, is to set aside the privilege of being God's "special people" (1 Peter 2:9, NKJV) to act as a servant and become obedient until death *to that way of Christ*. This will cause a school community (or any other community) to taste and see the blessings of trust in God (Psalm 34:8).[14] Individuals may or may not in the end receive Christ, but they *will* taste and see Christ living in Christ-like people. I have an opinion about how Christian education would change if Christ *alone* were reflected in a *fully* covenantal way as the *highest* objective from which all other goals and objectives are derived. But I *know* that this approach reflects human thoughts that are captivated by the obedience of Christ (2 Corinthians 10:5).

"This is all good and lovely," some will point out with a dismissive wave, "but *we* are covenantal." Others will say, "*we* are missional." What the apostles said was this: "we are casting down imaginations, and every high thing that exalts itself against the knowledge of God, *and bringing into captivity every thought to the obedience of Christ*" (2 Corinthians 10:5, emphasis mine). Brothers and sisters, it's time to set aside the exalted notion that *covenantal* and *missional* are antithetical terms, and that one or the other is superior. Christ has all authority to rule everywhere, everything, and everyone *toward* the ultimate redemptive objective of the godhead, *with grace and truth balanced by love*. Our adherence to Christ's obedient way is work the Spirit uses to sift the wheat from the chaff (Matthew 3:11–12).[15] Obedience in reflecting a covenantal community (Acts 2:39a) that contains a missional element to those who desire to approach nearness (Acts 2:39b), produces the fruit of God's will in saving. Are we willing to acknowledge that fear-driven controls merely reflect human preferences about God's redemptive purposes?

I urge you to initiate secret-place conversations among spiritual leaders in your Christian school community. Start with this question "Who is *Christ* and what is *His* way of 'schooling' believers?" Christ *is* covenantal; without Him there is no covenant and no promise. And yet Christ has *always* left room in that circle for those who desire to draw near. Is Christ reflected in your Christian school, without fear, both to children of believers and to those of sojourners, as pictured in the Old Testament and fulfilled in the New, where His way is presented as *the balance of love in grace and truth*? The balance of love will wax in grace and truth, as the felt need for control wanes.

> "Do not blaspheme the worthy name of Christ. If you want to fulfill the law of Christ, you will do well by *loving toward* neighbors as you have been *loved toward* by Christ. But if you have respect of persons, *loving toward* one and not another, you are committing sin, and you believe

that justification can be earned by obeying the law, even though you yourselves cannot obey it. If you obey the law but disobey in one thing, you are guilty of disobeying the whole law." (James 2:7–10, paraphrase mine)

"Therefore be imitators of God, as beloved children. And walk in *agape*, as Christ *agapao* us and gave himself up for us, a fragrant offering and sacrifice to God." (Ephesians 5:1–2, ESV)

10

Excellence: Beyond Measure

"And yet I will show you the most (*kata,* toward) excellent (*huperbole,* beyond measure) way (*hodos,* manner of thinking, feeling, deciding)." (1 Corinthians 12:31b, NIV)

The word *excellence* is ascribed fuzzy-buzz prominence in describing achievements, socially favorable outcomes, and religious behaviors associated with the current or former students of Christian schools, as evidenced through the measurement of data. As an indicator of relative levels of dysfunction and dissonance in a fallen world, measurement of data is an effective activity. It does not, however, require a *Christian* educator to recognize that functionality and harmony are improved by actions in response to measurement. The presence and power of Christ (excellence) are better recognized based on what is *absent* than by the *presence* of achievements.

As an introduction to *Christ's* way, the apostle writes *kata huperbole hodos*, predominantly translated "most (or more) excellent way." The nature or quality of excellence may be clarified by restating 1 Corinthians 12:31b: "And yet I will show you the manner of thinking, feeling, and deciding toward that which is beyond measure."

Agape, elucidated in 1 Corinthians 13 as the way personified in Christ, evades quantification even based on the presence of such supremely desirable and measurable outputs as eloquent tongues, gifted prophecy, deep understanding, expansive knowledge, strong conviction, self-denial, and/or martyrdom (1 Corinthians 13:1–3).

If the pre-eminent objective of a Christian school is to develop students toward or in the direction of a manner of thinking, feeling, and deciding (way) that is entirely captive to the obedience of Christ (most excellent), then the leaders of this school—who are, in effect, measuring what is *present*—must be at least equally concerned with what is *absent.* While I support the pursuit of all appropriate and measurable achievements, according to God's provision, I suggest *first* a passionate and ongoing secret place conversation to determine whether those things that must be *absent* when claiming Christ as the motivator of the organization are *actually* absent.

All achievements in a Christian school can be measured *and also mimicked.* And though skilled mimics bring significant utilitarian value to the human experience, they fail completely to address the ultimate problem: "each person is destined to die once and after that comes judgment" (Hebrews 9:27, NLT). Every believing educator, whether boasting missional or covenantal origin, desires *more* than to be of utilitarian value. Favorable achievements, after all, can be found in any educational setting. I would advocate that the only way to do *Christian* education is with the intentional absence of the ubiquitous self-motivators of the corrupt. This will seem foolish to those who are wise in their own eyes (1 Corinthians 1:27).

Deep spiritual dysfunction has been exposed in Christian education, primarily when the emergence of a value-add culture began to shed light on mediocrity. As concerns about sustainability increased, two dominant responses emerged. One was the avid pursuit of best educational practices, other goods and services, and the purported verification of spirituality through measurement. The other response has been the deluded belief that cultural disinterest in Christian education constitutes persecution against Christians, resulting in a stoic resignation to what is perceived as organizational martyrdom.

The *motivators* of these two responses, stated in their extremes, could not possibly flow from devotion to Christ because they fail to confess and repent of the spiritual dysfunction that led to mediocrity in the first place: namely,

Christ *and* . . . . Confession and repentance are non-negotiable precursors to putting *Christ alone* back in His rightful place. The very acts of advertising excellence or self-proclaiming martyrdom indicate the dominating involvement of motivators other than Christ. Spiritual renewal is always inside out—never outside in.

I won't take time to write about the many measurable qualities that must be *present* in the Christian school, such as those enumerated in 1 Corinthians 13:4–7 and Galatians 5. There is already a plethora of valuable "how to" books describing not only what must be *present* in schools per se but more particularly in a *Christian* school. The propensity toward checklists, processes, and prescriptions (outside in) in an attempt to self-reflect excellence or spirituality is highly overactive in the contemporary human psyche. Instead, I want to focus briefly on what must be *absent* in individuals who follow a Christ-like way—and therefore absent in the organizations they lead. Christ reveals these succinctly in Matthew 5:3–5.

In these first three Beatitudes the hearer is pushed toward a thorough examination of the inner self. First, those who are poor in spirit belong, as citizens, to the kingdom of heaven (Matthew 5:3). In the presence of God they have an attitude that is *absent* self-will of any kind, knowing that they have no means of access in themselves into the kingdom of heaven. Christian schools widely claim that they will save, transform, or make a difference in this world or usher in to the kingdom. It is the tragic and misplaced self-confidence of sin that boasts in the power of human efforts and educational knowledge to ensure the efficacy of any of these "ways" to, or even toward, the kingdom of heaven. *Christ's way was absent self-will.*

Second, those who mourn are the ones who will find comfort (Matthew 5:4). Mourning inevitably follows the absence of self-will. When confronted with a Holy God the mourner experiences sorrow for both personal and corporate sin; *absent* in this mourning is any idea of self-worth in terms of "goodness that earns relationship with God" apart from Christ or any notion that self can find comfort in self. Christian schools widely celebrate achievements, call them excellent, and hope these accomplishments will render them worthy and attractive. There are grand and copious celebrations over outward achievement in religious and other activity—but very little sober discussion of sin, confession of and repentance for, which alone can lead to lasting comfort. The wounds of constituents are lightly dressed. *Christ's way was absent self-worth.*

Third, those who are meek will inherit the earth (Matthew 5:5). In the absence of self-will and self-worth (again, as pertains to earning relational status with God), the meek exhibit the *absence* of self-protection. Having, by grace, arrived at an accurate knowledge of themselves, they respond to God and neighbor in love, as though they have never been hurt and considering others of more importance than themselves. Christian schools are prone to invest heavily in constructs of control in order to self-protect their safety or self-interest—sometimes bending the truth, sometimes defensive, sometimes self-isolated, and sometimes rationalizing in pursuit of this protection. *Christ's way was absent self-protection.*

It may be that my description of what must be organizationally absent in Christian education—self-way, self-worth, and self-protection—induces shock in an ecumenical environment that has been drinking human-centered Kool-Aid for decades. Keep in mind that I am focusing on "emptying" self not in a call to unrealistic and ungodly self-abasement but because I believe the "filling" of self has been over-emphasized and human-centered, resulting in an unbalanced view of love toward God and neighbor. If love is to be balanced, half the weight must be brought to bear on the "emptying" component. The Bible promises filling with the presence and power of Christ alone, *through emptying*, which is diametrically opposed to what natural humanity thinks about the path to success.

It seems preposterous that the absence of inordinate self-will, an inflated sense of self-worth, and self-protection would result in an inheritance first of the kingdom of heaven and ultimately of the restored earth, as well as in eternal comfort. But Christ adjures each of us, in effect, to "first compare yourself to God so that you know yourself *in truth*." After that you will be filled with the presence and power of Christ alone (*by grace*), enabling achievements based on love for God and neighbor. The goal of a Christian individual *is* to be emptied of self and filled with Christ. If several of those individuals are leading a Christian school, that goal will cause the presence and power of Christ to flow abundantly into all areas of school life.

The intrinsic difference between a Christian school and any other school has absolutely nothing to do with achievement, community life, or relational quality. A Christian school is essentially different in quality when it is led by people who are *new* people, *new* creations belonging to an entirely different kingdom. Christ's words about His kingdom and His people are more than pretty prose; they are literally true. This manner of thinking, feeling, and deciding confuses the rest of the world. If a Christian school is not a significant enigma to the surrounding public, the school may well be operating (at best) from a shallow understanding of faith.

The way of Christ was shocking and confusing to the materialistic and militaristic Jews who presupposed that the man Jesus would lead the charge toward a victory for their kingdom. Christ says in effect, "I and my kingdom are not like that." Being poor in spirit, mourning, and being meek constituted a scandalizing contrast to those Jewish notions of what should happen. These qualities are also in stark contrast to much Christian church and school thought of today. The epidemic of thinking and advertising Christian saving, redeeming, renewing, overcoming, difference making, and many other ideals ostensibly *for* Christ is pervasive. The greatness of organizational intentions and plans *on Christ's behalf* is a significantly popular but tragic public message. What if *this* message were to be broadcast instead: "not by might, nor by power, but by my spirit" (Zechariah 4:6)?

The prevailing thought in Christian education seems to be the opposite of what is indicated by the way of Christ. "Blessed ones" are the reverse of those who have confidence in their own organizations, powers, gifts, abilities, institutions, and other measurable works of humankind. The way to strengthen a dysfunctional spiritual foundation in a Christian school (or anywhere else) is to examine the innards of leadership and lose the self-way, self-worth, and self-protection. If measured and material achievements of any kind are not constructed firmly on a selfless foundation in truth, they are not built on Christ alone. He alone is excellent, and His power and presence will do abundantly more, *by* Him *through* us, as opposed to *by* us *for* Him.

Christ's excellence is evidenced in the obedience that necessitated His being emptied. "Let this mind be in you, which was in Christ Jesus . . . who made Himself of no reputation, and took the form of a servant, and was made in the likeness of men; he humbled Himself, and was obedient to death, even the death of the cross" (Philippians 2:5–8). Within the highly favored but absolutely unmerited state of regeneration, believers are called to function with a disposition toward the self that reflects Christ's disposition toward Himself. It is my considered opinion, based on observation, that Christ's disposition toward Himself is poorly reflected in Christian education as an organizational whole. And therefore it is *not* excellent, regardless of how many measurable achievements may or may not be boasted.

The power of Christ alone, through the operation of the Holy Spirit, fuels functionality *toward* the absence of human depravity (self, self, and self). An organization that is led to walk in the obedient way of Christ *only*, in and toward a manner of thinking, feeling, and deciding, *will be* excellent. In other words, a Christ-*only* organization is known first and foremost for what is *absent*, not for what is advertised, boasted, or achieved. In such a place it would be irrelevant who is *enrolled* at the school but highly relevant who is *leading* the leaders toward the absence of ubiquitous corruption.

In the interest of clarity, let me quickly interject a couple of ideas I'm *not* positing. First, that Christian schools should not measure. Rather, I'm suggesting that measurement of data is an inappropriate way to evaluate or boast *excellence* in a Christian context. I advocate measuring anything that is of integral value to the educating of children in order to improve the function and harmony of the teaching and learning cycle. I further suggest holding all professed Christian educators accountable to measuring while *first* engaged in vigorous "secret place conversations" that drive the self toward the way beyond measure.

Nor am I implying that all believers, by dint of their status in Christ, are excellent educators. Rather, I'm suggesting that Christian educators truly so named are demonstrably driven by the way of Christ (the excellent One) to improve the functionality and harmony of their craft; to self-analyze; and, most importantly, *to possess the spiritual maturity to transparently recognize and address the fallen nature at a deep and selfless level, rather than by outward actions and achievements*. Further, I would insist that the aforementioned—especially the italicized portion—describes the *only* appropriate candidates to begin or continue working in a Christian school.

Ponder briefly the level of craftsmanship that must have been present in the carpentry work of the excellent One during His earthly sojourn. Love toward God and humanity, driven by the standard of Christ as a motivator, will result in the presence of measurable fruits of every kind, according to

God's will and for His unique purposes. Simply stated, if there is no fruit the motivator isn't Christ.

I have no doubt that Christian educators think very highly of Christ. Sadly, they also seem to think highly of themselves *apart* from Christ, and to measure themselves by standards other than His excellence, which in turn allows for boasting. I have already suggested that secret place conversations will lead toward the dismantling of artificial controls and the emergence of a fully covenantal community driven by the balance of love rather than by dominating fears. Now I am adding that the balance of love in grace and truth *constitutes* biblical excellence because it leaves no room for the aggrandizement of self.

> "Arrogant religious people want a sign, and arrogant worldly people want the wisdom of the world. But those that are called by God want Christ, the power and wisdom of God. This is because the foolishness and weakness of God is wiser than the wisdom and strength of people. Take a look at yourselves, brothers and sisters; there are not many wise, mighty, or noble people of the world called to God in Christ. This is because God has chosen foolish and weak things in the eyes of the world to confuse the wise and strong of the world. He has chosen low and despised things, even things that are *absent* among people (grace and truth) to bring down things that are *present* among people (self and sin). He does this so that no people are able to give themselves glory when they are standing in God's presence. But you are in Christ Jesus, whom God has made to be our wisdom, righteousness, sanctification, and redemption: so if you are boasting, boast in the Lord." (1 Corinthians 1:22–31, paraphrase mine)
>
> "And this I pray, that your love (*agape*) may abound still more and more in real knowledge (*epignosis*, precise and correct knowledge of ethical and divine things) and all discernment (*aisthesis*, perception by the senses and the intellect of ethical matters), so that you may approve (*dokimazo*, test, examine, prove, scrutinize, recognize whether or not a thing is genuine) the things that are excellent (*diaphero*; spoken of things that carry through, last, or are of importance), in order to be sincere (*heilikrines*, pure when unfolded and examined in full light) and blameless (*aproskopos*, having nothing in self that causes stumbling) until the

day of Christ, having been filled with the fruit of righteousness (*dikaiosune*, condition or state acceptable to God) which comes through Jesus Christ, to the glory and praise of God." (Philippians 1:9–11, NASB)

11

Exagorazo Hemera

"Therefore, be *mimetes* (imitators) of God as beloved children, and *peripateo* (progress in your life's way, making use of opportunities) in *agape*, just as Christ *agapao* and gave up his life for us, as a fragrant offering and sacrifice to God. Look carefully, therefore, how you *peripateo*, not as unwise but as wise; *exagorazo* (making careful and sacred use of every opportunity to buy back the time), because the *hemera* (days until Christ's return) are *poneros* (full of labors, annoyances, hardship, and of an ethically evil condition)." (Ephesians 5:1,2,15,16, paraphrase mine)

In the first ten chapters of this book I have attempted to describe a renewed way *to be* in Christian schools. The biblical directive for Christian educators has not changed (Psalm 78:4; Ezekiel 47:21–23), but the world has changed drastically from age to age, and now at a rate more rapidly than ever before. At this particular time Christian educators have a unique opportunity to present themselves as "the epistle of Christ [written] not with ink, but by the Spirit" (2 Corinthians 3:3). In other words, to imitate Christ alone is to walk wisely, as a living letter, while redeeming the time.

A spiritually sensitive gaze into the contemporary landscape will expose opportunities to present Christ while imitating His way, and renewed emphasis on Christ alone will sprinkle the world with savory salt and stab piercing light deep into the growing darkness. It is my suggestion that, in lieu of hand wringing (or hiding and blaming), Christian educators above all others recognize themselves to be equipped with the tools to face the realities of the changed world and *exagorazo hemera*. Whatever God chooses to do with that faithfulness, He will do. Courage isn't the absence of fear but the belief that something else is more important than our fears—the something else in this case being imitation of Christ in order to redeem the time we've been given.

With that in mind I'll suggest five (of many possible) ways in which Christ-mimics could present themselves as living letters from Him in the context of a graciously unapologetic school community. But first I'd like to mention a truth whose corresponding lie has deeply deluded Christian thought. History is *not* an uninterrupted flow of progress. It is growth and decay, advance and retreat, progress and regression. For the child of God it's a continual struggle between the old self being worshiped as god and the new self moving forward in the direction of the supremacy and fullness of Christ as all in all. *For a soldier of the cross this conflict can only be played out on the battleground of one's own heart, in seeking to mimic the way of Christ in the sight of the world and in the circumstances in which one has been placed.*

1. Consider the recent shift from modernity to postmodernity that has resulted in general acceptance of challenge to any authority. As the pendulum swings from rigid order toward inevitable chaos, believing leaders in Christian education have a unique opportunity to present Christ's reign as supreme commander in the hearts of leaders by demonstrating His determinative order and direction, regardless of what subordinate authorities may be doing. In the face of growing disorder they have the privilege of presenting Christ as the *only* One who can bring order to inner chaos and keep the inner beasts at bay; of living inside out rather than outside in. The most difficult form of government is *self*-government—a battle that must be fought before any other can be effectively engaged.

2. As the industrial age has rapidly given way to the age of information, individuals are being driven apart by global communities that favor broad but shallow alliances as opposed to earlier times of connection close to home and deeply. A heavy emphasis on electronic information and communication as relationship produces a deep undercurrent of loneliness and disillusionment. Those charged with leadership in Christian education must seek to know and

love *all* constituents (even the distasteful ones), just as their own self has been known and loved by Christ. This requires painstaking, thoughtful, and precise relational interactions that "judge nothing before its time" (1 Corinthians 4:5; Ecclesiastes 3:17) and "give without expecting to receive" (Acts 20:35). Out with uniformity for the sake of control. In with the minute, specific, and individual care of Christ toward all those the Father has given Him (John 17). Upon the Christian school God has conferred educational responsibility for the children both of believers and of those He is drawing from afar off.

3. Christendom as a whole, and with it denominations of every kind, ebbed while post-Christendom was flooding in. Biblically religious organizations must "own" some of the force behind this flood. Where Christ has been preached but His way has not been lived, widespread self-righteousness and hypocrisy have left in their wake myriads of wounded people, whether direct or indirect casualties. For those in a wounded state who end up utilizing Christian schools, everything believing leaders communicate nonverbally speaks more loudly than whatever they say aloud. It is urgently necessary for their walk and talk *first* to harmoniously represent Christ as the head of the Church universal and invisible before depicting Him as the head of any particular institution.

4. As the production initiative faded and consumer awareness grew stronger, the impetus to produce and provide morphed into what constitutes in my opinion an almost obscene focus upon receiving and getting. What will I contribute to this community? has given way to What will this community contribute to me? The result is an insatiable hunger and thirst for fullness in conjunction with a frantic effort to assuage that felt need through material goods, secure situations, religious behaviors, intellectual supremacy, fulfilled dreams, and the like. Contentment has been relegated to the background, almost to the point that it has become a foreign concept even among many contemporary church types. We can find in this an opportunity to lead by presenting Christ in the context and at the center of a contented life—not in a pattern of being anxious to see far down the road, overly concerned about the next step, eager to choose our own path, or consumed with the worry of future responsibilities, but in following the Shepherd day by day, quietly and unalarmed.

5. Finally, religious identity has waned as spiritual exploration has waxed. The world has turned, as it were, into a marketplace of spiritual vendors.

Shoppers traipse from booth to booth seeking salve for sore souls. Like zombies, neither dead nor alive, they endlessly and mindlessly wander and grope. The graciously unapologetic school stands as a booth in this marketplace at which educators can present Christ in undaunted, vigorous life in the face of any challenge. It is as though their lives are shouting, "Whatever doesn't kill moves me in the direction of Christ; whatever *does* brings me immediately face-to-face with him. It's a win-win situation!" It's quite conceivable that spiritual zombies will be moved to ask the reason for this inner hope (1 Peter 3:16).

Considering only these five opportunities for *exagorazo hemera*, I think it's clear that many children will be left behind by a Christian education that fails to prepare them to mimic Christ in the context of the rapidly approaching global fallout. Such students might become (or their leaders might be) effective professionals, hard workers, well-educated, and moral church attenders, philanthropists, and the like. But are these results, good as they are, *all* that is desired from the efforts of Christian educators? Does it matter only that students and leaders are well-educated, convincing mimics of accepted religious behavior? I have no doubt we'd all prefer to see them become well-educated, zealous imitators of Christ.

Zeal is yet another fuzzy-buzz word. David's fervor alienated him from religious ceremony and drove him to pray for vengeance (Psalm 69), Elijah's passion produced prayer that resulted in three years of famine (James 5:16–17), and Christ's ardor resulted in righteous anger (John 2:13–17). The zealous of today seem only to entreat the Lord for more people, more money, more religious observance, bigger buildings, and better circumstances—more of whatever it is the would-be zealots define as desirable. But God's kingdom doesn't translate to what people decide they need or want in order to do the things they've defined as what God needs or wants. According to God's will zeal may or may not result in any of the things people desire or define because zeal is a desire for *God Himself*, not for a particular outcome in terms of temporal circumstances. God's kingdom is spiritual (Luke 17:21) because Christ resides in hearts. May the *heart* of Christian education, through its leaders, be purged before becoming fully lukewarm, a state of being toward Christ that will cause it to be "spit out" (Revelation 3:16).

Courage and zeal are needed to live as an inside-out exposition of Christ's epistle, written on hearts by the Spirit—exposing natural man's invisible assumptions outwardly and answering them visibly and undeniably through the role and presentation as imitators of God in Christ *alone*. Much has changed in the world. And much has changed in the church, home, and school. But Jesus Christ, His Word, and His way never change. Even now His presence and power are able to transform leaders of schools into wise imitators of Christ who *exagorazo hemera*.

> "Jesus Christ is the same yesterday and today and forever." (Hebrews 13:8, NASB)
>
> "For from Him and through Him and to Him are all things. To Him be the glory forever. Amen." (Romans 11:36, NASB)

12

Admissions Policy Statement

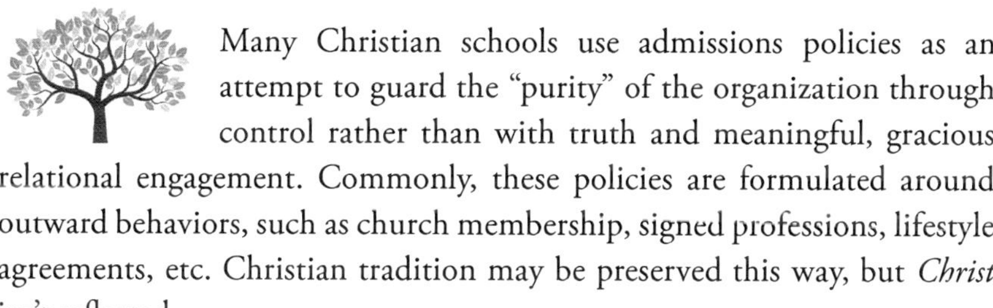

Many Christian schools use admissions policies as an attempt to guard the "purity" of the organization through control rather than with truth and meaningful, gracious relational engagement. Commonly, these policies are formulated around outward behaviors, such as church membership, signed professions, lifestyle agreements, etc. Christian tradition may be preserved this way, but *Christ* isn't reflected.

Absent an intentional Christ-like way of being, faith-based organizations develop according to group norms, and the limits and boundaries of the organization result from dominant fears. Sacrifices extend to boundaries of self-determined will, and righteousness to the self-attainment of law. The focus is on what people are doing and saying instead of on what Christ has *already done and said.* This seductive error has been prevalent throughout all of His-story. I'm suggesting an unequivocal rejection of fears about what will happen if leaders of the Christian school don't seek control (as opposed to establishing order in grace and truth), allowing for the power and presence of Christ to increase in our schools even as we decrease (John 3:30).

The grace in admissions policies is without reserve when it erects no ideological barriers to who may or may not be the recipient of an education at the school. This trusts God's will in terms of whom he will draw. Truth is without apology in admissions statements when it is positively and clearly delineated up front. This approach trusts God's Word to attract and repel. All those who are drawn to apply will do so when fully aware of the ramifications. School/home partnerships rest on mutually responsible agreement to a statement of faith, an admissions statement, and a parent/student handbook. Following is an admissions policy statement sample that is both gracious and unapologetic. An editable copy of this policy statement is available at www.balancepointalliance.com.

ADMISSIONS STATEMENT

Christian School X (CSX) was founded and is governed by those who believe that children of believers must be educated according to God's Word, the Bible. This community of believers welcomes enrollment to any who desire to attend for other reasons, provided the personal choice to enroll follows an understanding of what will be taught and accompanies an agreement to follow the guidelines set forth in the Parent Student Handbook, as expressed in this Admissions Statement and in accordance with the Statement of Faith. Each enrollee of this community is welcomed in Christian love through a reflection of the Grace and Truth of Jesus Christ (John 1:14). All families must read and sign this admission statement yearly, indicating understanding of, and willingness to submit to, the teachings stated below:

1. CSX is committed by faith to be governed by, led by, and educated through spiritually mature Christian believers as board members, administrators, teachers, and support staff.
2. CSX is committed by faith to the interpretation of all subject material in light of a biblical worldview. In broad summary: a sovereign Creator and lawgiver, the fall of man, and redemption in Jesus Christ alone.
3. CSX is committed by faith to teach, wherever it is developmentally appropriate, and in connection with subject material and all

community life, that the moral law of God is the only right standard of living. This includes, but is not limited to:

a. A biblical definition of love as acts and interactions that demonstrate, at all times, that each human being is of infinite value based on having been created in the image of God. This is true even in light of the fact that each human being is corrupted by the fall into sin. *This prohibits CSX from teaching or interacting, by action or word, as though uncontrolled anger, hitting, bullying, ridicule, sarcasm with intent to hurt or demean, isolation, control for the sake of control, etc., is acceptable in God's eyes. This list is not exhaustive.*
b. A biblical definition of sexual purity as human sexuality that is limited to the intimate physical union between one woman and one man, bound in marriage by a vow. *This prohibits CSX from teaching or interacting, by action or word, as though premarital, extramarital, and same-gender sexual unions; pornography of any kind; bestiality; polygamy; heterosexual co-habitation without marriage; excessive or inappropriate public displays of affection; excessive or dominating immodesty and/or indecency, etc., is acceptable in God's eyes. This also prohibits participants in the CSX community from engaging in public displays of affection (PDA), whether heterosexual or homosexual, that suggest, promote, or display intimate physical union. This list is not exhaustive.*
c. A biblical definition of human life as the immediate result of conception and as being of infinite value. *This prohibits CSX from teaching or interacting, by action or word, as though abortion were acceptable in God's eyes. In connection with this, CSX will proactively teach, when developmentally appropriate, sexual purity within the confines of marriage and seek to train students in an understanding of the vast and deep responsibility associated with sexual intercourse and the procreation of human life.*
d. A biblical definition of integrity as interactions that demonstrate, at all times, an understanding of and response to God's ownership and distribution of all things, whether in public or in private. *This prohibits CSX from teaching or interacting, by action or word, as though*

cheating, lying, stealing, sneaking, manipulation, rebellion, etc., is acceptable in God's eyes. This list is not exhaustive.

e. A biblical definition of human identity that is rooted in the "awe-some and wonderful" work of God in the intentional formation of each human being in the womb (Psalm 139:14) and the unique position of humans, above all other creatures, as image-bearers of God (Genesis 1:27). *This definition of identity prohibits CSX from teaching or interacting, by action or word, as though attempts to alter the fundamental structure or representation of the human body were God-honoring choices. This includes gender changes; cross-dressing; and structural changes, such as snake-tongues and horns, excessive tattooing, and body mutilation. This list in not exhaustive.*

f. A biblical definition of order as mutually responsible agreement on a set of guidelines that reflects the order and design of God's creation. This order ensures the progress of the whole child toward the peak of his or her potential. The guidelines for order at CSX (for the academic, behavioral, emotional, and spiritual growth of students) are outlined in the Parent-Student Handbook.

g. In summary, the mission of CSX requires that biblical truths, held in faith by the founding, governing, and teaching participants of CSX, be taught and integrated into all learning as the final and absolute authority on all matters of faith and life.

I, the undersigned, have read and understood, and agree to submit my child(ren) to biblical teaching at CSX without seeking to promote or pressure any members of this community with any personal beliefs, lifestyles, or opinions that undermine or adversely influence the faith beliefs as . . . .

(1) outlined above in this Admissions Statement or
(2) found in the Parent-Student Handbook
(3) or in the Statement of Faith.

Should I become dissatisfied with the faith-based teaching at CSX, or find myself no longer able to engage in mutually responsible agreement, I commit to peacefully seeking an educational institution whose foundation and beliefs are not in conflict with my own beliefs and understand that failure to do so will result in expulsion. (*End policy statement.*)

When a Christian school's way of being is graciously unapologetic, personal fears about the relative "badness" of behaviors and ideologies become irrelevant, because Christ is being taught without apology *to* school constituents *in school*, and the choice to remain under this teaching *without open opposition* rests with the learner or his/her parent(s) and/or guardian(s). The same guidelines apply to standards of conduct within the school community. It is exceedingly gracious and truthful to deal consistently and carefully with the multitude of issues that invariably arise (discipleship) within the lives of students and families. As pointed out previously, Numbers 15:15–16 states that one ordinance will apply to both the home-born and the sojourner (*ger*).

The sample admissions policy statement lays a foundation for daily practice and process. The next chapter deals with application of this policy to practice and process.

13

Admissions: What, How, and When

"And I saw something else under the sun: In the place of judgment—wickedness was there; in the place of justice—wickedness was there. I said to myself, 'God will bring into judgment both the righteous and the wicked, for *there will be a time for every activity, a time to judge every deed.*'" (Ecclesiastes 3:16–17, NIV, italics mine)

Responses to the Admissions Policy Statement (APS) recorded in chapter 12 tend often toward skepticism: "in real life that doesn't work." If the objective is to screen out worse sinners or minimize indelicate situations *before the feared outcome materializes,* this approach will not work. But if the objective is to communicate clearly ***what*** will be taught to everyone, all the time; ***how*** responsible relational partnerships are defined; and ***when*** the partnership will be actively dissolved, it will work—if, that is, "real life" in the context of Christian education is defined as *courageous school leaders living by the standard of Christ in secret place conversations in the direction of grace and truth balanced by love.*

Another frequent response is patronizing disinterest, because "real life" has mistakenly been defined by criteria such as insufficient enrollment, poor response to data, apathetic families, scarce resources, etc. – and *not* connected in any way to spiritual malaise by those respondents. Sadly, temporal considerations (synonymous with "real life," so defined) can never be separated from spiritual considerations because faith is inextricably linked to reason. Seeking to artificially disconnect the two is a cowardly way to check all the outer boxes in an attempt to avoid inner sickness. Christ says, though, that "the healthy don't need a doctor, but the sick do. I have not come to call the righteous, but sinners to repentance" (Luke 5:31–32, HSBC). Christian schools described by their leader(s) in terms only of temporal challenges and responses, while placarding all the Christian stuff onto the surface, are being led by wolves wearing sheep's clothes.

Given that context, the balance of this chapter provides a brief glimpse into the *what, how,* and *when* of the APS at work in real life in a Christian school.

Re-enrollment

A parent/guardian of every child signs the APS every year during the process of re-enrollment. In addition, every 7th–12th grade student studies and signs the APS in Bible class at the beginning of every year. Dialogue with students is focused on the *what, when,* and *how*. With those filters in mind the reader may want to reread the APS in chapter 12. Whenever there is a concern, for any reason, about the APS or its understanding, the document is printed and discussed openly with the concerned party(ies).

Initial Application

As part of the initial application process for any given student, a parent/guardian signs the APS *and* is required to provide answers to four basic questions:

1. What church are you affiliated with?
2. What would you like your child to learn about God?
3. What are your three highest priorities regarding the total education of your child?
4. Why have you chosen Christian School X for your child?

The answers to these questions are reviewed at the time of every new application and, where appropriate, trigger a face-to-face meeting initiated by the school. During this meeting the *what, how, and when* of the APS are read aloud and discussed in depth. The leader of the meeting does not dig for information on the personal beliefs, affiliations, and lifestyles of the applicant beyond what the applicant offers; does not debate over differing views; and does not defend, rationalize, or apologize for the faith positions held by the school. In *this* meeting the leader isn't concerned about what an *applicant* believes or lives or thinks. He or she focuses on communicating what the *school* believes, how the *school* will operate, and under what circumstances a partnership would be dissolved by the *school*. Every applicant is then able to make a well-informed decision.

This meeting comes to a close with some form of the following statement: "Christian School X is non-negotiable about our faith beliefs, and we welcome your attendance. Are you comfortable committing your child to training in a school that believes and actively teaches these things (*what*); operates as described (*how*); and actively parts company under the circumstances described (*when*)?" If yes, enrollment proceeds. If no, it doesn't. It is usually obvious which choice a family will make long before this wrap-up question is asked; the point is to reinforce that the school has put the choice in the lap of the applicant by speaking confidently, clearly, and honestly about the non-negotiable elements of participation at the school and then waiting for the outcome to come out.

Open Opposition

Students and/or families that cannot or will not maintain mutually responsible participation within the *what, how, and when* boundaries of the APS most often *self*-eliminate, whether initially or eventually. But in rare cases it is necessary to actively remove openly oppositional participants from the school community. Chapter 4 briefly discusses the perversion of law against the vulnerable, and this is a primary reason to avoid rigid processes when discipline progresses toward dissolution of the partnership. However, there are several helpful principles to guide interactions in the course of progressive discipline.

First, the severing of a relationship in a graciously unapologetic school setting could be defined in different words as "*the definitive end of a discipleship relationship where the only remaining path of grace and truth is to take an immovable stand*." The relationship of Jesus with Judas is a poignant example. Jesus *knew* the outcome and yet was obedient, full of grace and truth throughout the relationship. Jesus waited, in other words, for the *outcome to come out*. In discipleship, leaders often *suspect or fear* a particular outcome, and that fear leads to sinful contributions of their own in the direction of the relational breakdown they already perceive as inevitable. In other words, they seek to control others by using the gospel of sin management before the (expected) "coming out" of the opposition.

Second, I define a "disciple" as *one who is in a learning relationship with believer(s) who reflect Christ*—rather than the more common conception of a *younger believer in a mentoring relationship with an older believer*. The common conception may assuage the fear of unfavorable outcomes in the relationship, but it limits discipleship to training in the "goodness" or "badness" of outward behaviors because presumptions of belief have already been concluded based upon outward actions. (Allow me to clarify that there is no causation, and only minimal correlation, between outward acts and receiving the gift of faith.) Ponder the prevalence of presumptive declarations about who is, and who is not, saved within the Christian school context. Why is it so difficult to rely on the effectual inner working of the Spirit and the Word, while satisfied with regard to the self alone with the obedience to reflecting Christ? A believing reflection of Christ is based upon Christ, not on an opinion regarding the disciples' state of salvation.

Third, escalating discipline should evolve from swift and initial examination of the *self*, only then advancing to slow and deliberative decisions and actions in response to the oppositional party. Love demands that self be taken out of the equation *first* so that Christ may be reflected without interference or unnecessary complication. The leader is called upon to *reflect* Christ, but the Spirit of God alone determines what a disciple will *see* of Christ's reflection. If that relationship between the discipler and disciple is legitimately severed through expulsion, the disciple should find no authentication for reasons or excuses based on the leaders' failures. Imagine Judas saying "It's Jesus' fault." Judas was clearly responsible for his own actions. But so are we. Christ did not leave His initial band of disciples, nor does He leave us, the recourse of turning anywhere but inward to find motivations for their own behavior. Neither should we.

Fourth, God designates children in the Christian school as disciples of grace and truth by virtue of the fact that He has drawn them there, into relationship with those reflecting Christ. Every situation that requires discipline, *involving any child in the school*, is in reality one of opposition, whether passive or aggressive. The vast majority of interactions in Christ-like discipline result in growth of some kind, even if only behavioral. Discipleship requires careful, thoughtful, painstaking, prayerful, self-less, and grueling work, and a desirable outcome is not always forthcoming. The fact that some discipleship interactions will end like that of Jesus and Judas does not relieve any leader in Christian education of the responsibility to enter deep and meaningful discipleship relationships with every student and family God calls to the Christian school community.

Case Study #1

An initial application contained the following answers to the questions asked in the application process:

1. Congregation Church of Whoville.
2. That God loves everyone.
3. A good education. That he (the son) loves everyone. That he (the son) is happy.
4. We heard good things about the school.

These answers triggered a meeting due to concern over widely publicized positions of the denomination cited and based on a lack of depth in the remaining answers. In the course of the meeting it was discovered that the parents were a same-sex couple, full communicant members of the Congregation Church of Whoville, and that their child was the product of insemination.

Following is the gist of what was communicated in the meeting: the son is welcome in Christian love, which is defined by the way Christ treated those for whom He died and by the Truth He teaches them, as understood and believed in this school. The beliefs at this school are contrary to your beliefs, and our way of life is contrary to what is taught in your church. The beliefs of the school will be expressed respectfully and without apology in connection with developmentally appropriate content material and in relational interactions. If beliefs of the school are expressed in a demeaning way, the school will address the *way* the belief was expressed, but not the *content.* Attempts to undermine or adversely influence the faith-based positions of this school will result in a severing of the relationship. The Statement of Faith and the APS were read and discussed candidly. Several scenarios of possible difficulty were posed and discussed.

The gist of the outcome is that the parents chose to continue with admission. The child spent three academically fruitful years at the school, and the eventual reason given for withdrawal was financial. Gracious relationships established by teachers led to conversations of Truth with the parents. The couple was ignored by some parents at public places, such as birthday parties and the grocery store. To my knowledge, however, the child was not ostracized. The two moms were to my knowledge compliant and respectful in all interactions with teachers, administration, and all others, and the child had no discipline issues that would have required administrative involvement.

On one occasion a group of concerned parents requested a meeting to discuss the school board and administration's position on same-sex couples and on admissions policies. The APS was read and discussed, and the *what, how,* and *when* were defined. This group of parents was satisfied with the answers but also wanted assurances that teachers had been, or would be, trained to have graciously unapologetic conversations in the classroom when and where needed. Such training is part of the administrative responsibility.

It was deeply painful for the school when the couple withdrew the child. Two teachers in particular had invested a great deal of time and effort in building a gracious relationship with the mothers and the child, which had led to numerous deep and transparent conversations in truth. These teachers had come to know both women as individuals who were desperately groping for solid ground, continuously learning but never coming to a knowledge of the truth (see 2 Timothy 3:7).

Whatever God does with the grace and truth of Christ that have been reflected, He does. I rest in the assurance that the school obediently sought the way of Christ with these very restless souls.

Case Study #2

The son (I'll call him Jimmy) of professing Christian parents was enrolled in his 7th grade year after experiencing what was described to me as bullying. By the 9th grade Jimmy was claiming in the presence of peers to be a "Satanist" and "bisexual" (his words). Upon first hearing of this I had a conversation with Jimmy, which boiled down to this:

Me: Jimmy, did you tell other students you are a satanist and bisexual?

Jimmy: Yes.

Me: *Are* you a satanist and bisexual?

Jimmy: I am a satanist because people misunderstand what it's about—it's really about love. And I am bisexual because I'm attracted to both genders, but I'm not sexually active.

Me: Thanks for your honesty. I don't know what it is that people fail to understand, but I want *you* to understand what I am about to say: you are at a Christian school, and at this school we teach God's Word and present God and Satan exactly as the Bible says they are. We also teach that all sexual intimacy outside marriage between a man and a woman is sin. Everything contained in the Bible is absolute truth. If you talk about your beliefs or way of life in any way that undermines or adversely influences anyone at this school, you will not be permitted to stay. Do you want to stay at this school?

Jimmy: Yes, I won't talk about my beliefs. I want to stay here; everyone here is really nice to me.

Me: You may talk about your beliefs as part of a respectful intellectual discussion in the classroom, where the teacher decides what is respectful and appropriate—not you. You may write about your beliefs in written assignments where they are appropriately connected to the assignment—and again, the teacher decides what is appropriate. You may not proselytize or promote your beliefs with other students. And you may not undermine any beliefs held at this school or expressed by students of this school. (We discussed several hypothetical scenarios.)

Jimmy has been compliant within the boundaries I had given him. I believe I had two follow-up conversations over a two-and-a-half-year period—both on minor issues—and in both cases Jimmy was compliant and followed my instructions. Jimmy is drawn to the Bible teacher and seeks out many after class discussions. He is quiet and somewhat distant, engaging shallowly but warmly with other students—all of whom are aware of his beliefs, as are his teachers. Others treat him kindly but firmly with respect to Christian positions, and Jimmy does not challenge that. Many students and teachers have expressed that they have prayed for him regularly.

Jimmy is withdrawing at the end of his 11th grade year. He does not state why, but one of his parents said, and I quote, "The school ruined him; when he came here he was a perfect, cookie-cutter Christian." These words were spoken as though "perfect, cookie-cutter Christian" were a good thing. Perhaps therein lies the bedrock of Jimmy's significant challenges in life. In any case, the outcome is deeply painful for Jimmy's teachers, who have extended themselves far out on the limb of grace. As of the time of this writing they have received nothing in return other than scorn from the parents. I value these teachers highly, and watching them in these interactions has taught me more about Christ.

Whatever God does with the grace and truth that were reflected to Jimmy and his parents—He does. I know beyond a doubt that the school obediently sought the way of Christ with Jimmy and his family—who are now choosing to self-eliminate.

Conclusion

I used these two examples to highlight the fear of entering partnerships when religious preconditions are not in place to pre-assess or protect against feared outcomes. In a graciously unapologetic way of being, the school will without doubt encounter conversations, situations, and relationships that prove to be painful and uncomfortable, and sometimes seemingly unbearable. Allow me to reiterate: biblical courage is *not* the absence of fear. It is the conviction that reflecting Christ is more important than fear.

I could write a whole series of books containing examples of the regular and peaceful path of Christian fellowship with the vast majority of families in the school. And I could fill at least one book with examples exhibiting obvious and radical transformations among families—some originally professing Christ and others not. But the relational interactions of a Christ reflector are not about the outcome; they are about captivity to the obedience of Christ, while waiting for the outcome to come out.

> "When a man's ways please the LORD, He makes even his enemies to be at peace with him." (Proverbs 16:7, HCSB)
>
> "For nothing is concealed that won't be revealed, and nothing hidden that won't be made known and come to light." (Luke 8:17, HCSB)

14

Finding Fear and Choosing Love

". . . For as he thinks in his heart, so is he. 'Eat and drink!' he says to you, but his heart (leb, *inner man*) is not with you." (Proverbs 23:7, NKJV)

The word "leader" in this book refers interchangeably to believing parents, board members, administrators, teachers, and support staff. The common objective for all of these leaders in terms of a Christ-like way could be stated as *the progressive identification of fears, accompanied by loving movement toward God and the students, in conjunction with their families, in the context of education.* This way cannot be typified by any particular set of behaviors, verbal confessions, or qualifications of people; it is characterized by growing self-awareness, resulting in a progressively harmonious inner and outer self.

With growing self-awareness comes the recognition of inner fears and their connection to outer acts and interactions. This recognition presents the inner self with the same choice Christ made perfectly in his interface with sinners: *to love freely and purposely, regardless of the consequence to Himself or the badness of sinners.* This conscious choice comes down either to loving

God freely, through obedience, regardless of the consequence to self or the badness in others, or to continue in the fearful self-reliance of corruption. (Parenthetically, this is different from the New-Age choice of self-love, where the self has become aware that reactions dominated by fear are generally not advantageous in the pursuit of a pleasant earthly life.) A Christ-like way chooses *selfless* love.

I pause here to articulate what I believe the Bible says about the freedom of choice. Free will is a real state that follows salvation. Believers in Christ are free to follow: free to obey, free to suffer, free to rejoice, free to abound, free from fear's oppression, free of sin's dominion—free, free, free! But the kind of choice that *precedes* salvation must be identified by a different noun: "bondage." *Before* a relationship with Christ, and *until* the heart is changed by the Spirit, *every* choice is bound completely to the corruption of sin. It is only *after* the work of the Spirit makes one alive in Christ that every choice is bound to Christ's perfection, allowing the individual to be liberated from fear. Alive in Christ, believers *can and will,* of their own volition, progressively, and without fear, choose Christ's way over their own (Galatians 5:1; Ephesians 2:1–10). Dead in sin, people can't and won't choose Christ or His way.

I have found that I cannot apply grace and truth, balanced by love, to others until I have sought and then grappled with my own fears in secret place conversations. Sometimes this is simple, but in other instances the process is complex, difficult, confusing, infuriating, heart-wrenching, and more. Recognizing or identifying fears, followed by acknowledging and engaging with them, is progression toward a Christ-like way; this is not a hard-and-fast, single-answer solution you "get right" in order to check it off in a box. The secret in the "secret place of the Most High" *is* to uncover and relieve personal fears "under the shadow of the Almighty" (Psalm 91:1, ASV).

Following is an actual example. This email excerpt and its answer might provide insight into what it means to discover fears and choose love. Bear in mind, though, that every individual leader making concrete plans to recognize fears and choose love will be directed by the *Lord* in the steps (Proverbs 16:9) they must take toward greater and greater discovery of a fearless self in the context of a loving Lord.

"Just Mean Nasty Little Kids"

". . . [M]y concern is that by taking on undisciplined and basically just mean nasty little kids, that the 2–3 bad apples spoil the whole bunch . . . if you know what I'm saying" (excerpt from a parent email).

The problem for me was that I knew *exactly* what he was saying—and that knowledge caused blinding anger in me, a state in which I cannot reflect Christ. My primary fears in this instance boiled down to two: fear of personal failure and fear for the children struggling with the problematic behaviors. A couple of salves that calmed these fears were my knowledge of God's perfect plan and of His sovereignty in the accomplishment of that plan. I am responsible solely to reflect the Christ-like way of grace and truth. And even though the email messenger used words that were deeply distasteful to me, made unsubstantiated assumptions, and implied absolute *un*truths, I heard an important message: it is never a waste of time to provide progressive discipline (discipleship) for the children and families whom God places under my care, no matter how difficult it may seem at the time.

Before I had dealt with myself I would by nature have hidden or shifted blame, just as Adam had done. In practical terms this hiding and blaming manifests in such behaviors as "white-knuckled" polite responses, anger, defensiveness, and rationalization (or other forms of passive or active aggression). None of these choices would have arisen from love toward anyone. The choice to love demonstrates itself in *setting aside personal fears, with their natural responses, in the favor of grace, in order to articulate the naked truth that alone has the power to relieve the fears of the other.* This is exactly the manner in which Christ loved sinners: He loved the Father first and then, in obedience, those whom the Father had given Him (John 17).

There were multiple fears (on his own part) and errors (on the school's) implied by this father's reactive email. But I chose to focus on two in particular because we, like Christ, teach progressively. First, the originator of the email feared that undisciplined child(ren) would ruin the Christian school environment for his child(ren)—an environment that I knew him to hold dear. Second, I believed that he was afraid to ask the straightforward question that would have been appropriate: "*How does the school (or you) deal with students who are struggling with behavior issues?*" This father instead opted for the oblique approach, shifting blame onto the "mean nasty little kids" in lieu of risking my offense.

My response was twofold. I first scheduled a full staff discussion around the questions "Are we dealing well with discipline?" and "Where could we improve?" Second, I proceeded to answer *the* question I intuited to underlie the indirect email approach. My answer rose from a deliberate choice to reflect "in the most excellent [possible] way" Christ's love toward me—a love in which He "bears all things, believes all things, hopes all things, endures all things." I chose to personally *bear* the sorrow and anger, *believing* that this father would learn a better way to love and *hoping* for an opportunity in God's design to speak directly to the ignorance I felt myself obliged to *endure* at this time.

I sent the email below:

"I and the teachers are committed to acting toward every child with loving discipline in a progressive way, because each child has come to the school as a result of sovereign design. We cannot guarantee when and what behaviors will occur, or what challenges the Lord may put in the path of any particular child or family. But we promise, without reserve, to deal with all behaviors in a path of progressive discipline that produces progressive growth in behavior, or eventually ends the relationship because we have neither the skills nor the resources to bring progress to the openly oppositional behavior.

"We are called to love each one of these children. We promise to interact this way with real knowledge, making no judgment before its time, and while considering the unique needs of the particular child and of the group as a whole. Please pray for us and hold us accountable by asking questions whenever you are uncertain of the facts of a situation. We need this because we are the same as all of our students in that we were conceived and born in sin. If you would like to meet with me or any particular teacher(s) to discuss this in detail, please let me know, and we will make arrangements at your convenience." (End email communication.)

Question: Is the sin demonstrated in this parent's email statement less "messy" or less egregious than that of any given sojourner? In my opinion, and based on my experience with other, similar situations, it is equally egregious but exceeds in messiness because the light of Christ is badly darkened within the Christian school by an expression like this from one who professes Him.

One of the indescribable beauties of true obedience, which has its beginning under the shadow of the Almighty, is that Christ *leads* applications of selfless love in the presence of such obedience and that the Spirit *follows* to establish and strengthen the heart in *agapao*. However, when we opt instead to take the "broad path"—to live life on the surface, avoiding the pain of discovering our sinful fears—we will surely miss "the depth of the riches both of the wisdom and knowledge of God" (Romans 11:33) in Christ.

The relational quality of every leader in the Christian school must begin with intentional and progressive activity in the direction of identifying fears and choosing love. This is markedly different from limiting ourselves to teaching and integrating content with a biblical worldview (knowledge) or talking about the Word and Christ during conflict or discipline (understanding). The bottom-line approach I'm advocating is to *live* that knowledge and understanding selflessly as a reflection of Christ *alone* (wisdom). If Christian school leaders in any strata of the organization cannot be led progressively to do this, I would suggest that Christian education is for them an inappropriate vocational choice.

Without intentional pursuit of the balancing influence of love, Christian education as a whole will continue to reflect a polarized tension between two paths: either a way of convenient grace and rigid truth or one of easy grace and flexible truth, all defined by something other than Christ. This is not to suggest that education in either case will not be done well; the question is whether it will be done in a *Christ-like way*. One can indeed do education without Christ; numerous institutions excel in this endeavor. The crux of the issue is whether *Christian* education can be accomplished in the absence of a Christ-like way.

> "As You have sent me into the world, in the same way I have sent them (those whom You have given me for eternal life) into the world." (John 17:18, paraphrase mine)

15

The Battles of the Board

"And Moses called to Joshua and spoke to him in front of all Israel, be strong and of a good courage, because you must go with these people to the land that the LORD has promised to their fathers to give them; and you will cause them to inherit it. And the LORD is the one that goes before you; and the LORD will be with you; and the LORD will not fail you or forsake you; fear not, and do not be discouraged?" (Deuteronomy 31:7–8)

What if the board of a given Christian school were making organizationally formative decisions while holding on to fears that Christ alone is not enough? Such decisions might result in outcomes like allegiance to a particular systematized doctrine rather than to the Lord it represents; an emphasis on 'free-will' choice and saving souls; or self-assigned objectives like earth restoring and justice seeking. If teaching Christ in content and process is the primary objective of an organization, an ongoing battle to identify fears and progressively release them will become the primary battle of the board.

To avoid misunderstanding, allow me to make a few clarifying statements: I favor the study of systematized doctrine as a *tool*; I give thanks for *a will that has been freed* from the bondage of sin through the operation of the Holy Spirit; and I consider it *obedient* to work heartily in any application the Father assigns to me, including restoration or justice. The problem is not doctrine, choice, or service work. The problem is that the old self *prefers* to add something to Christ, fighting incessantly to make something, anything, *about self and what self does* instead of *Christ and what He has accomplished already.*

This human preference results in insidious and pervasive shifts in cause and effect. Factors like doctrine, choice, and service work become *causes*, and Christ Himself takes a position in our minds similar to that of Santa Claus, presumably delivering the *effects* of human goodness, as gifts. To combat this mindset, internally and then through open dialogue, has been the primary battle of believing life ever since Cain killed Abel. The issue is not that this battle will be won by any individual or organization; it's that Christian school board members as a whole seem *not to be battling* this human preference in decision making and direction setting.

Meaningful *spiritual* change in a Christian school begins with unapologetic dialogue around the boardroom table. Personal fears are to be set aside in grace, so that truth may bring relief to the fears of the group professing to love and trust God in Christ. I will proceed to offer a few examples of places in which some of these fears might be found. Bear in mind, though, that humans and their plans will be directed in their steps *by the Lord* (Proverbs 16:9) toward greater and greater discovery of fearless board leadership. "And my God will supply all your needs according to his riches in glory by Christ Jesus" (Philippians 4:19, NASB).

Control

Following a seminar on board governance intended to encourage meaningful order rather than blind control, a board president responded as follows: "That would be great if it were possible; the problem is that there are no administrators who can be trusted."

If in fact there were no trustworthy administrators, this would have implied the need for heart-wrenching dialogue about the viability of the school. If the then current administrator had in reality been untrustworthy, this should have stimulated dialogue about termination. But if this ridiculous statement was indicative of a need for control—then fear was a dominating motivator on this board. All of the possibilities implied by the statement should have provoked vigorous, truth-filled dialogue, resulting in decisive action(s). What actually happened was nervous rustling, no dialogue, and no resulting action.

A failure to engage in deep and challenging dialogue on any Christian school board will result in a "control walk" that is the polar opposite to "love talk"—because fear and control are the defaults of human corruption, while love and freedom are possible only in Christ. The reason to battle "control walk" is that it is *opposite* the way of Christ. Obedience demands that ongoing efforts be expended in the direction of Christ's way.

Unity and Clarity about Why

In a tense discussion about behavioral policy, one board member was pushing for "rigid rules and no tolerance." A second favored "guidelines broad enough to allow growth and learning but narrow enough to promote order and safety." A third board member asked, "Why are we serving on the board of a Christian school?"

The first answered, "I'm here for the same reason *everyone* is, to protect my children from bad influences!" The second followed with, "That's not why *I'm* here! That's not even possible!" The third chimed in, "Apparently we don't know why *we* [the board members] are *here* in the boardroom—because *that* has nothing to do with *specific* parents and their personal reasons for enrolling their children."

Such differences of opinion are often treated as preferences, and the "why" fluctuates with the coming and going of the strongest personalities on the board. I believe that unified clarity around *the one legitimate* answer to the "why" question—to teach Christ in content and process—is a biblical imperative (as opposed to a preference). Other preferences, beliefs, or personal agendas ought to be challenged in loving, truth-filled dialogue to the extent necessary to provide unity and clarity on that simple, yet profoundly important, extremely powerful, and obedient objective.

Self-Assigned Causes

I have alluded to self-assigned causes several times already. Some examples that come to mind include justice seeking, creation keeping, culture redeeming, kingdom ushering, life transforming, social inspiration, difference making, soul winning, truth protecting, functioning as change agent, servant leading, or world overcoming. What *drives* these widely advertised (and humanly unattainable) causes? And *are* these causes in reality self-assigned?

A specious relationship will always exist between self-assigned causes and decisions; at play is a form of relativism in which "the right thing" is considered to be that which aligns with the self-assigned cause. Could the inconvenient truth simply be that Christian schools have adopted a number of causes *as primary* that should rightly be termed *activities in agapao* that should flow naturally from the primary cause of *being in the way of Christ*? Is it possible that this adoption soothes fears of sustainability? Or feeds pride in works Christ presumably *needs* people to do? Or self-reflects self-righteousness?

Consider this example from the promotional materials of a particular school. Students are described as "warriors advancing the Lord's kingdom." The school promises award-winning academics, arts and athletics, and thereby offers students the "opportunity to demonstrate God's love" as warriors. These warrior-students "take action, using time, talent and treasure," and when they are older they "will live lives of character, service and influence." They do community service, take initiative in worship, join clubs, and serve all over the world. As warriors "they move beyond the classroom" to "transform their own lives, our community, and the world."

In the masterful artwork of the promotional material, which evokes deep emotion and longing, Christ is positioned as the *spectator and recipient* of all this "doing." What the school *does* (inputs) and what the students *will do* (outputs) after attending this kingdom-advancing school together comprise the singular prominent feature. Also prominent—perhaps more so—are statements about who those students *are*. "I am a sculptor. I am an entrepreneur. I am a missionary. I am a mentor. I am a musician. I am an engineer. I am a servant. I am an author. I am a mathematician. *I am a warrior*." If anyone at this school is to find their "I am" identity in the One who says "I AM that I AM" (Exodus 3:14), this expectation is not stated anywhere in the promotional materials.

I don't know the intention, but this is the message I "heard" from a thorough review of all the promotional materials: "Come to this school because the success of the kingdom will rest on these students, through the efforts of the school; a believer or Christian (the materials use *only* the word "warrior") is defined by school inputs and student outputs; and Christ is a spectator and recipient of these kingdom-advancing gifts. I can only assume that salvation would be the reciprocal gift from Christ in his turn to the kingdom advancers, but this is—not surprisingly—not spelled out in the materials." Causes other than Christ might indeed build strong organizations (this particular school appeared to be organizationally strong), but other causes do not build *Christ-centered* organizations.

I shudder to think what students of this school are being taught about Christ. Graduates who think critically will know that they have not transformed and cannot "transform their own lives, our community, and the world." Graduates successful as "warriors" will find identity in religious behaviors and personal achievements, enjoying the spotlight of group norm. And graduates who struggle, for one reason or another, to survive the day, let alone to succeed as "warriors," will wonder how *this* Christ could possibly help them. I concede that Christ is not learned *because* a school "gets it right," but I'm asking board members to consider the possibility that the school they lead may be teaching a *different* Christ.

Where a school board does in fact lead in the way of Christ as the primary objective (cause), many activities in *agapao* will flourish (effect). But where a school board leads with self-assigned causes, *Christ* will not follow *the school board* for effect.

One Employee

Let's envision that the primary objective of a school board is to "teach Christ in content and process" and that this primary objective is driven by *agapao*, which in turn flows into ideologically consistent educational and organizational objectives; and that the board employs one person who is responsible to lead in fulfillment of the primary objective and be skilled in guiding the integration of all secondary objectives in day-to-day operations of the school. I'll call that employee the helmsman.

I heard a story a year ago from a Christian school board member. The story communicated popular organizational practices *du jour* in defense of a newly hired helmsman. In spite of my prompting, no evidence of deeper dialogue over the spiritual qualifications of the helmsman was forthcoming. A few days ago I heard a *new* story from the same teller, as though the previous had never been told. The school has experienced a significant drop in enrollment since the hire of the helmsman. The reason given by the storyteller was a "reign of terror," an example of which was the helmsman's requirement that everyone rise to their feet when the helmsman entered the room.

I use this example to make a point about the internal battles of the board, not about the qualities or approach of this particular helmsman. I cannot verify the details of the story, nor would I care to. It doesn't really matter, because the same story is often repeated with different details—the *happening truth* is the point. I addressed the happening truth to the storyteller, commenting, "When relaying details of this helmsman's hire, you gave no evidence of caring about spiritual leadership. Apparently you got exactly what you were looking for. And when the 'reign of terror' began, what did the board do about it other than tell stories to people other than the helmsman? I would suggest that *graciously unapologetic* dialogue, setting aside personal fears to erect a non-negotiable, Christ-like way as a standard for interaction, would either solve the problem or remove it from the school."

An unrelenting battle on the part of the board must be to find and/or develop men or women who have the *spiritual* capacity to do the job of helmsmen. Fear and control are not the answer. Nor is a shallow pseudo-spirituality that overlays world theory on leadership and organization with Christian words. The high, unyielding standard of love that balances grace and truth is the answer. Want better helmsmen? Hold and live the highest possible standard: a Christ-like way.

If the school were a ship, the single core objective would be the rudder, the school board would chart the course, the helmsman would steer, and the students would be precious cargo. Don't "do battle" with the helmsman; do battle with yourselves, board members, to provide leadership in a Christ-like way. If the board charts an unclear or questionable course, there can be no doubt the ship will drift based on any number of threats, now here, now there.

Before my colleagues at the helm of Christian schools retort that a spiritual approach is less than seriously professional or effective, please allow me to make two blunt statements. A spiritually mature helmsman who is ineffective educationally and organizationally is *an oxymoron,* because a spiritually mature helmsman would remove him or herself from any helm where they knew themselves to be ill equipped to steer effectively. Conversely, an effective educational and organizational leader who cannot defend, demonstrate, or promote a Christ-like way in all domains of education at a depth that exceeds biblically religious norms is steering the school toward spiritual destruction. It behooves Christian school board members to seek and develop a helmsman who is accountable for a fully integrated personal example and professional application of Christ's way through effective educational and organizational leadership—or release them to lead in other educational venues where Christ is *not* professed as all.

Conclusion

The battles of the board, if Christian schools are to be renewed in faithful obedience, will require more than the many excellent efforts already underway to improve school board functionality. I support and devote energy to these efforts. But alone they will fail to meet the objective of renewal, because the relentless preference of humans to earn or control will not go away until the Lord returns. This is very simply the corruption and curse of sin to which there is no antidote other than Christ alone. I repeat below what I have already said:

The fallen tree will be renewed at the root of Christ, and Christ alone. All believers throughout history are guilty of periods in which the paths of Christ *and something else* are chosen above what we perceive to be the higher-risk way of Christ *only.* It is following sincere repentance for that fundamental error that Christian education will move forward unimpeded on a path of spiritual renewal. The frenzied angst surrounding our hand-wringing discussion of "what to do" in order to "save" the nest ignores the reality that nestlings cannot rest in or learn to fly from any nest built in a tree whose trunk is compromised very near the ground and whose roots are rotting. Christ alone stands ready to restore the root and nourish the tree; the fruit of the promise follows obedience to the command.

"Christ is the image of the invisible God, the firstborn of every creature: for by him were all things created in heaven and earth, visible and invisible, whether thrones, dominions, principalities, or powers: all things were created by him, and for him: and he is before all things, and by him all things consist. And he is the head of the body, the church: who is the beginning, the firstborn from the dead; that in all things he might have the preeminence." (Colossians 1:15–18)

16

Helmsmen: In a Spirit of Liberty

"God, all that has come on us is just; because you interacted faithfully, but we have acted and interacted wickedly. Because our leaders have not kept Your law (*agapao*)." (Nehemiah 9:33–34a, paraphrase mine)

"Now the Lord is the Spirit, and where the Spirit of the Lord is, *there* is liberty."(2 Corinthians 3:17, NASB)

Christian education as a whole appears to be in a precarious spiritual position that would be understandable were we to conclude that the helmsmen have overwhelmingly allowed the law of *agapao* to take on a lesser role than that of fears. After all, a tenuous spiritual condition is in itself the effect of unaddressed fears; organizationally, this scenario places the helmsmen in a dangerous vice grip between the downward fears of the school board and the cares of the constituents rising upward. In spite of this real and present danger, helmspersons occupy the *most* critical organizational position from which to model the letting go of fear in order to lead in the way of Christ, exhibiting the spirit of liberty that results.

Loving God in Christ, and thereby surrendering to His way, is effectively tantamount to letting go of fears. In the spirit of liberty that results, helmsmen function as representatives of Christ in His offices. The prophet seeks to ascertain and communicate truth *without fear of the reaction*; the priest graciously sets aside self *without fear of personal consequences*; and the king makes and executes decisions rooted in love *without fear of error*. It's impossible to say whether others will follow suit within the organization, but one can certainly deduce that this threefold functionality reflects the obedience of Christ in His way of living and leading. It *is* possible to steer the ship in a dominating spirit of liberty without fear of reaction, consequence, and error: after all, "Where the Spirit of the Lord is, there is liberty" (2 Corinthians 3:17).

Perhaps readers will find it an oversimplification to assert that turning away from an image of the self as "good" in favor of finding *all* in the grace and truth of Christ is the singular hinge upon which the door to spiritual health will turn. If so, consider again that "in the last days, perilous times will come and men will be lovers of self." Ask yourself once again whether it is conceivable that professed Christians are in the main lovers of self rather than lovers of God—based on falling into the trap of holding to structural godliness (goodness) while denying the fullness of Christ, *the* all-sufficient power of godliness (2 Timothy 3:1–5). Addressing this question is difficult and even painful, but it's worthy of consideration if believing leaders are to be willing to set aside their fears in order to rest in Christ's way. This is especially critical in terms of their unique position of influence where Christ is being taught to the next generation.

The Prophet's Word (unyielding truth): seeking to discover and disseminate the truth *without fear of the reaction*.

A Christian school board president recently recounted his memory of an interview for the position of superintendent. He commented, "What I remember was the challenge the interviewee threw out to the board to 'stop advertising the school as "the premier education in Somewhere County."'" To honor the way of Christ as prophet, His Truth must be *told* by would-be and operating helmspersons regardless of the real or perceived consequences to self—an inconvenient truth that is not always recognized or internalized.

Reasons for the requested consideration were discussed between the interviewee and the interviewing board. At length the conclusion was reached that to advertise as "premier"' was at worst a lie and at best unsubstantiated. There was no measurable data to support this claim academically and no biblical definition of "premier"' to objectify its understanding. It was concluded as well that neither being "premier" nor boasting of that status is an appropriate primary objective in a Christ-centered school. Even if a Christian school could be demonstrably verified by some appropriate definition to be premier, this would not in itself be a desirable promotion of the way of Christ. If enrollees are to be attracted, let them be attracted to sound education, integrated throughout by the way of Christ. (If sound education is *not* happening—the way of Christ is *not* being well integrated—fix *that* first.)

In this particular case the school board was facing some highly destabilizing organizational times, leading to fears of extinction. These rational concerns led to the unspoken assumption that the survival of this particular school was God's specific will (presumed cause) and that marketing "premier education" in response constituted the appropriate "what-to-do decision"—despite sacrificing verifiable truth. Desperate times call for desperate measures, as they say. This scenario is highly understandable; similar situations may be expected among believers until the Lord returns. But who will have the courage to promulgate the truth that relieves these kinds of fears in the organizational setting of Christian schools?

In this case the interviewee (now helmsman of the school in question) was willing to declare the truth that alone had the power to calm the fears of the board—that teaching Christ is the objective of the school, that Christ will protect and maintain the school, that Christ will drive excellence by biblical definition, and that *believers are required only to cast down high imaginations to take captive every thought to the obedience of Christ.* The Truth will not yield to human fears, change in favor of presumed causes, or fail to advance God's will and plan.

The term "unyielding truth" is not to be understood as an invitation to speak one's mind incessantly and without appropriate editing. Quite the opposite: a helmsperson must do far more listening than speaking (Proverbs 29:20) in order to discern *how*—and *when*—the word of truth must be fitly spoken (25:11–13). When this person does talk it must be with skillful wielding of the Word.

The Priest's Sacrifice (unlimited grace): sacrificially setting aside self *without fear of personal consequences.*

Over the last several years I've heard two frequently repeated concerns. The first is that the heads of Christian schools are "run off," "burned out," or "fired" on an average cycle of every three years, and the second that a rapidly diminishing number of willing and qualified leaders are available to fill the role of helmsmen in Christian schools.

Assuming that these concerns reflect an actual dilemma, one might deduce that the predicament is due to the dangerous vice grip created by fear-driven environments. But it might *also* suggest some failure on the part of helmsmen to be clearly and consistently reflective of Christ. When they find themselves in the role of having to reflect the priesthood of Christ on a ship that cannot or will not turn from fear-driven governance, how many helmsmen don't cluelessly enjoy the voyage until they find themselves thrown overboard, as opposed to making an intentional transition to steering a Christ-centered ship? In other words, how many are consciously willing to sacrifice *themselves*?

A colleague in Christian educational leadership recently relayed a personal story pertaining to the "control and fear politics" leading up to a leadership transition. The change was perfunctorily announced and cut short the agreed upon length of contract, and all decisions about *when*, *what*, and *who* had been made behind doors that were closed to the then helmsman leader. This brand of politics, which had been going on for seven years, now adversely affected the helmsman himself. Assuming that the account was accurate, the absence of candid dialogue between the board and administrator over a period of years had resulted in the *truth not being spoken by either.* The unaddressed motivations, fears, and/or concerns over this period of years can only indicate a pervasive self-focus and serve as examples of *grace not being extended by either side*; the entire scenario is reflective of self-love on the part of both the board *and the helmsman.* Self-love is contrary to the way of Christ. In fact, I would go so far as to posit that the absence of *selfless* love is tantamount to the presence of hatred, regardless of how grace and truth are outwardly mimicked.

Ponder with me a few questions in this connection. Following an extended period of control- and fear-dominated politics, why do helmspersons not change ships? With what degree of grace and truth do helmspersons typically address fear and control when they identify it? Is it sufficiently satisfying to receive a paycheck and self-protect when experiencing the vice grip of a fear- and control-driven environment? Are the politics of fear and control acceptable provided they do not create a personal problem for the helmsman? Are the deep incongruences between the functional definitions of the terms "Christian" and "governance" not noted by the helmsmen prior to their being thrown overboard? If not, *why* not?

How might the situation change if school boards operating in the context of control and fear were *unable* to retain good administrators for more than a few years? I'm envisioning a scenario in which the "few years" constituted a period of time during which the helmsman was actively seeking to establish a spirit of liberty by applying grace and truth in love. Or how might the picture change if Christian school boards were consistently confronted by helmsmen willing to self-sacrifice by their insistence upon steering in the direction of Christ alone? Might it be true that the typical helmsperson enjoys the privilege without the responsibility—even though nothing about this dynamic reflects the leadership of Christ?

The term "unlimited grace" is not to be understood as though it were an invitation either to live without boundaries, shifting with the fickle demands of human leadership, or to "tough it out" while remaining consistently "nice" and hoping for the best. Quite the opposite: a helmsperson *must* set uncompromising boundaries based on the grace and truth of Christ alone. It is variations *outside* those bounds that initiate the necessity of helmspersons acting as immovable walls in yielding self while wielding truth. Anything outside the parameters set for us by Christ alone boils down to a matter of preference, convenience, or expedience—allowing for the flexibility of Gumby. Acting like Gumby, according to personal advantage, comes naturally, a reality that behooves us to spend a lot more time in prayer and meditation about *when* it is appropriate to act as an immovable wall.

The King's Balance (*Agapao*): making and executing decisions rooted in love *without fear of error*.

In terms of salvation history, it was only the ultimate decision of Christ as King that resulted in believers becoming fully good in the eyes of God—that rendered them triumphant in fulfillment of God's plan. This good news means that the helmsman, as a representative of Christ the King, is essentially relieved of any pressure to "get it right" in organizational decision-making. What a comfort to know that the King's decisions, work, and plans cannot be offset or overridden by any decision a helmsman makes. Leadership that is representative of Christ the King causes progressive movement toward confident and sober-minded decision-making without fear of error, *despite the knowledge that every human decision will invariably contain error.*

The most powerful word of truth I have ever heard in connection with decision-making was the three-letter word *yes*. I found myself standing as it were on the edge of a cliff with no doubt that to back up would be to deny Christ but to step forward would be to effectively initiate a free fall through a seemingly endless void. So I angrily asked, "What do you suggest I decide—to step out into a void?" My father's reply was a simple yes. But that yes followed years of his declaring that God in Christ *alone* will make Himself responsible for all of the consequences into which obedient decisions may lead—because on account of Christ "the everlasting arms are underneath" (Deuteronomy 33:27) to catch us.

I tell this story here in the hope that the Lord will use it to en*courage* the helmsmen who have been uniquely placed as representatives of the kingship of Christ in these perilous times—times in which kingly decisions often appear, and frequently are, dangerous. "So do not fear, because I am with you; do not be dismayed, because I am your God; I will strengthen you, I will help you, I will uphold you with my righteous right hand," declares the prophet in Isaiah 41:10. Christ alone *is* God's "righteous right hand." Am I asking my fellow helmsmen to step off the edge of a cliff? As it pertains to Christ *alone* in the context of false gospels that preach Christ *in conjunction with* something else, yes—in the assurance that the everlasting arms really are underneath.

The insidious and pervasive lies that the "goodness" of Christians is demonstrated by their ability to decide the "right" thing and that to sin or not to sin is a free choice render confident decision-making and consistent execution elusive qualities among organizational leaders in Christian education. Again, this is partially due to the nature of the vice grip. But it is also due to the "goodness" lie that the self really *wants* to believe—that particular decisions (following the one truly good decision to "accept" Christ) will demonstrate human goodness, achieve human success, or ensure fulfillment of God's plan to the extent it can be humanly understood. This is how Christian communities end up believing themselves to be empowered to make the "right" or "wrong" decisions in the minutia of daily life and in the causal direction of lives and organizations—in essence attributing to themselves power that belongs only to God in Christ.

The only fully right decision one can make is that of letting go of the fear of condemnation in favor of trusting Christ for all things. This decision is fully right *only* because it can be fully credited to the operation of the Spirit and the work of Christ and not at all to the person. Every other decision, whether preceding or following this critical choice, is influenced by some level of corruption in the person and within the context of the worldwide weight of the curse. Consequently, instead of the accountability for letting go of fear to trust in Christ for all things, fear of the "wrong" decision forces evaluation on the basis of indicators that lie outside the bounds of personal or organizational fears. Letting go of fear opens a channel into which the spirit of liberty drives a confident examination of all the possibilities, both inside and outside the bounds of personal or organizational fears.

Only the person at the helm can truly evaluate the parameters of a given decision. I can honestly concede that I have never to my knowledge made a fully "right" decision, either for myself or for the organization I lead. But I can say without doubt that where I seek the utmost for His highest without fear of error *He* steers toward *His* port, and the everlasting arms are always underneath the dangerous waters on the voyage *toward Him*. "These things I have spoken to you," reassures Jesus, "so that in Me you may have peace. In the world you have tribulation, but take courage; I have overcome the world" (John 16:33, NASB). This tribulation goes beyond "bad" people giving "good" people a hard time; in fact, that isn't what it's about at all. It's the believer's old self doing battle with the believer's new self *in Christ alone* in the face of any fears. This reminds me of the life of Jacob after Peniel—of the remainder of a lifetime of limping along as a prince in the company of God (Genesis 32:22–32).

To those representative kings of organizations who are steering with a desire to do the utmost for His highest without fear of error, I offer some personal commitments one might prayerfully consider making while in secret place conversations. I have found them to be invaluable in steering my own decision-making toward a Christ-like way, and for me they have resulted by grace in a dominating spirit of liberty—but often for others as well.

1. Extend to others what you have received from God.
2. Require of *self* what God requires of self. *Teach* others by any means available and appropriate what God requires.
3. Hear incoming messages detached from the sender's mode of delivery, and speak outgoing messages in consideration of the receiver.
4. Seek multiple counselors in unsettling decisions. In urgent circumstances, act swiftly and decisively, without fear, while trusting God.
5. "Own" and submit to any failure or inability that enters your consciousness, whether intentional or unintentional, outward or inward, with friend or foe, to the appropriate parties.
6. Drive decisions as far down as possible into organizational structures, empowering others to make choices in a spirit of liberty.
7. Begin conflict resolution by asking *What have I done?* before *What have you done?*
8. Prioritize and execute all that is possible within a given set of circumstances and in a given time frame. If necessary, throw everything else off the wagon for another days' load.
9. Resist the temptation to seek a "magic fix." There is no such thing as a permanent solution other than in Christ alone.
10. Every morning go to God and let go of fears. Every day do your best and forget the rest. Every night review, renew, *and rest* in Christ alone.

Conclusion

The *happening* truth for Christian schools is a more biblically accurate variation of Edmund Burke's famous quote, "All that is necessary for evil to triumph is for good men to do nothing." (Parenthetically, how is it that "good" men can do nothing in the face of evil? And that evil can triumph if in fact Christ is reigning?) Variation: "All that is needed for Christian organizations to crumble spiritually is for helmspersons to do nothing courageous in the face of fear." Love toward God, and then the neighbor, yields self and wields truth, always driving the ship into the narrow channel of Christ *alone*. Or, in the words of

Christ, toward the "narrow gate," found by only a few, leading to the difficult way that follows the only viable and ultimate Way (Matthew 7:13–14).

The boundaries of a believing life are drawn with the hand of grace so that inheritance with Christ alone is the truth that frees one to embrace the lesser pain of earthly life while seizing the blessings of greater life in Him: *a spirit of liberty*. In a spirit of liberty, then, lead on! Christ *alone* wields the power to set a prodigal helmsman on a homeward path, and He is certainly able to re-chart the course of a renegade ship according to His will—when the helmsmen is obedient to the command of steering toward Christ alone.

> "For though I am free from all men, I have made myself a slave to all, so that I may win the more." (1 Corinthians 9:19)

17

Overseers and Underlings: Abundantly Exceeding

> If you love those who love you, what fruits will result from your labors; even the people you despise do that, right? And if you welcome only those with whom you have a close association, what remarkable thing are you doing? Doesn't everyone do that, even those you despise? You must *perissos* (abundantly exceed) because your heavenly Father is *teleios* (perfect, complete). (Matthew 5:46-48, paraphrase mine)

In *Christian* education, the overseer and underling relationship is where grace and truth get down to the nitty gritty; where the battle between fear and love is fought; where the old and new in Christ are constantly wrestling. Students answer to teachers, teachers to administrators, coaches to athletic directors, and helmsmen to a board, and board members to each other. Every one answers to someone. And except for students, everyone is responsible for the oversight of someone. Thus we have an organization filled with overseers and underlings.

The privilege of authority as an overseer carries a responsibility to provide accountability to the underling. Exercise of this responsibility is uniquely pivotal in *Christian* schools because the communicated impetus in *that* learning environment is a Christ-like way (*agapao*). As an overseer, the educator is responsible to progressively discover and reduce *other* loves (*eros, phileo, and storge*) from dominating in the school environment so that *selfless love* is continually freeing the learning environment of fear-inducing obstacles. And to do so, in itself, is to love the underling with selfless love. This is how educators *perissos* (abundantly exceed) as Christ urges in Matthew 5.

Whether or not any of these other loves are appropriate in other settings is not the issue. The point here is that they must be intentionally reduced in relationships of authority and accountability within the Christian school. *Eros* teaches love as worship of the creature; *phileo* that it is give and take; and *storge* teaches love by association. It is not that students don't learn from these loves—it's that they learn something contrary to *Christ's* love in an environment whose sole objective is to teach (school) Christ (Christian) in content and process. The talk of content is denied by the process-walk of one whose other loves obscure the love of Christ.

The balance of this chapter contains examples which have been chosen to illustrate a point. Some are extreme and unusual, others seemingly innocuous and common. But all of these "other loves" show up in a myriad of ways throughout each and every day, in every one of us and all of them, whether extreme or seemingly innocuous, have the power to badly obscure the teaching of Christ when left unaddressed.

Eros—Identity and Value

Identity. I knew a particular teacher for eight years. Initial concerns with her were the absence of objective standards, unstructured dialogue as primary teaching methodology, and the extreme "love" or "hate" reactions of students toward her. (Some students oft repeated, "I love her!" because their personal dysfunction was co-dependent with hers, interlocking perfectly with her perceived identity; these students could never lose. Other students oft repeated, "I hate her!" because their personal dysfunction clashed with hers; unable to feed the perceived identity.) The overseer of this underling did not act with authority or provide accountability, leaving *eros* unaddressed.

The teacher continued in the same way over the period of years with students proclaiming they "hated" or "loved" her, and content learning was predominantly limited to what I would call accidental. Then one day the teacher called in sick on the same day as a particular high school student called in sick. The mother of the student came home unexpectedly and found the teacher and student spending the day alone in her home. The unique vulnerabilities of this particular child, sexually assaulted at a very young age, were perfectly suited as prey for the teacher whose sense of identity was inextricably linked to the "love" that students had for her. It was at that point that the teacher was fired.

The *happening* truth in this story is that *eros*, even though recognized by the overseer, was permitted to grow and fester like a puss-filled boil until it burst and spewed filth over any talk of *agapao*. *Anti*-Christ was taught more profoundly than whatever had been taught in words in this particular Christian school during this period of time. It was taught by the administrator *failing to provide accountability* and more obviously by the teacher; the worst consequences falling on the child. Failure to provide progressive accountability where one holds the responsibility of authority is a result of *self* love. When fears are set aside to speak the truth that has the power to set someone free, it fixes the problem or it eliminates the danger to students. The teacher, at the beginning of the eight years and following, was not loved. As a parenthetical reminder, the overseers *first* responsibility is to protect the children, not the teachers. I say this because the overseer in this story stated often that her job was to protect teachers—she protected neither.

"But for the grace of God there go each of us," because *eros* has a unique presentation in every human. When the meaningful accountability of *agapao*, balanced by grace and truth, are progressively applied without pre-judgment it solves the problem *in Christ*, or it removes the problem from the Christian school. The aforementioned is true because the power of Christ's love played out in real life *forces* hidden darkness into the open light. This is where, again, the power of Christ brings repentance or push-back (attracts or repels).

Value. In an exit interview, distraught parents described their child's anxiety when attending school; this anxiety had risen unassuaged throughout the year. According to them their son's teacher had called him names, ridiculed him publically, and ignored his academic needs throughout the year. The parents themselves had felt mistreated at the times when they had expressed their concerns to the teacher.

Perceptions during exit interviews are often inaccurate, exaggerated, or outright wrong by nature of the fact that they have usually been "held" and "stuffed" for the whole year. It is common that exit interviews begin with "I was trying to be kind (or not bother you, or gracious, or patient) so I didn't say anything about this before." But I have never found these perceptions to be made up of nothing. Strong perceptions do not arise in a vacuum—all overseers must pay attention to them and at the same time make intentional efforts not to judge things before their time.

A lengthy conversation with the teacher in question followed the exit interview and several alarming statements were made. One statement, when discussing academic achievement was, "all my other students are good students." (aka: this student is bad.) Another in response to "how does this student learn *uniquely*" was, "I don't know, my *other* students work hard." (aka: this student is lazy.) These two statements alone indicate that at least some significant portion of the anxiety has cause within the teacher.

After hearing much defensiveness and rationalization with considerable counter-attack—I paused and asked, "if we set aside all the child's, parent's and my issues for a moment (which we can deal with later)—what could be done differently *in your classroom and your teaching* that could have helped this child feel emotionally safe and ready to learn?", and she blurted out, "I don't know! I'm a *good* teacher—if the child is filled with anxiety and can't learn it's not my fault."

Please give the human default toward personal valuation serious thought. Spend a full day intentionally *not* using the words "good" or "bad" with children. Or when providing accountability ask the "sinner" to name the sin in detail that necessitated this particular accountability. Everyone in the Christian school is able to call themselves a general sinner, but very few can or will describe a particular sin. This is often because what they have done or not done throughout life has been valued as "good" or "bad"—and the result is often a coping mechanism that is an artificial system of labyrinthine boxes to check in order to feel the temporary relief of being the "good child."

For Christian educators this is a particularly serious problem because it causes the next generation of children to associate their value with performance: academically, behaviorally and/or spiritually. Or I should say *fails to teach them something other than performance based value*, which is a default in all of us. Using valuation as a teaching methodology is immediately damaging to the low achiever, but ultimately more so to the high achiever—who grows up believing that everything he does is "good." Some examples are good and bad grades; good choices and bad; good behavior and bad behavior; and "good" worship (which we often call spirit filled) as evidenced solely by outward acts such as the raising of hands, swaying, musical performance, and eloquent speech. Evaluation of *truth* in the worship not so much. Everyone has *infinite* value as an image bearer of God and *no-one* has *self*-worth in the presence of a Holy God. The tension that arises around this inconvenient and unyielding truth is relieved in Christ *alone*.

Eros dominates when the underling must act or interact in a particular way in order to confirm a belief about a particular identity or value in the overseer outside of, or apart from, the value found as an image bearer of God and redeemed in Christ. Those who are able to act and interact to confirm the belief are favored; those not able suffer passive or active aggression. Essentially, *eros* is a desire to be as God while manipulating vulnerable people to worship the idol that self has made of self.

Phileo—Equality and Reciprocity

Equality. The mother of a fatherless high school student had asked a teacher to spend time with her son to provide guidance. At the point that the teacher expressed discomfort to me about the situation I asked, "What is the fear that underlies your discomfort?" The teacher expressed his fear that the mother presumes that he will "save" the child from his errant way. The teacher had been meeting with the student on Saturdays. Since the Saturday interactions had begun without ground rules, inappropriate equality had been communicated to the student causing a sense of entitlement and the mother did indeed have inappropriate expectations about the teacher-student relationship. The point at which the teacher became uncomfortable was the point at which he realized that equal social standing was the only basis to continue the encounters.

The encounters began in response to the mother's request *without communicating the appropriate objective and time-frame of the interaction.* Overseer and underling relationships remain on appropriate footing (unequal) when overseers communicate the boundaries of objective and time-frame clearly in the beginning of an endeavor, and then repeat as needed in accountability. This gets messy when overseers do not understand their own responsibility in a relationship containing authority, and unsure of themselves, communicate boundaries poorly or not at all. This makes for a lot of confusion on the part of students who are already a part of a generation that rejects authority. A well-written syllabus and a clearly communicated set of behavioral expectations *that are consistently followed without subjective valuation* are great simple examples of boundaries that contain objectives and time-frames.

Reciprocity. Following are a few of the many variations of emotionally manipulative statements that echo from the halls and classrooms of Christian Schools across North America on a daily basis. All these statements teach the same underlying message: "I like you (or not)—because you are 'good' (or 'bad')." And when this is communicated by a representative of Jesus Christ, it communicates something far worse, "God saved you (or didn't)—because you're good (or 'bad')." Reciprocity and valuation are opposite sides of a coin. The experience of reciprocity is felt by the "good" underling, and valuation by the "bad" underling.

"It makes me happy when you're 'good.'" Is a child responsible for an adult's emotional stability? How afraid might this child become about the adult relationship when he is 'bad'? Does the process message (emotional instability in the adult) match the content message (Christ is my all)? Is the objective of teaching appropriate behavior to keep adults happy? Imagine this learning objective, . . . *students will behave in a way that keeps adults happy.*

"*Jimmy,* God is *crying* right now—stop it!" Is Jimmy responsible for God's state of being? Is obedience the result of guilt manipulation or the equivalent of behavior management? When Jimmy learns about sovereignty and transcendence, will he already be thoroughly manacled in a prison of fear and control? Will he view God as maniacal, frivolous, and fickle? If emotional manipulation succeeds in molding Jimmy's outward character, we'll call him "Christian." If it fails, some professed Christians will respond with smug superiority because they made the "right" choice that Jimmy didn't make.

When the child of reciprocity is an adult, they say things like, "everything I've done, I've done to make your life easier", with deep emotion and lots of tears. I heard this just yesterday from a teacher that was being challenged to seek underlying reasons for consistent relational breakdown between herself and colleagues. A labyrinthine system of reciprocity allows her to perform seemingly perfectly in all external ways. I quickly followed up on the statement with, "what do you think makes you feel responsible for the ease or difficulty of my life?" I love teachers very much and it grieves me that in her home, or in her Christian school—someone burdened her with the fear and control of reciprocity. Reciprocity has no place in a Christ-like way. None. The overseer is responsible to use truth to seek a spirit of liberty, and grace to set aside the fear of real or perceived personal consequences for the sake of the underling. That is selfless love.

Storge—Preference and Prejudice

Preference. All of us *have* preferences. I remember yesterday when I preferred not to deal with a staff issue. I remember when I preferred not to listen to a forty minute tirade from an angry parent. I remember when I preferred my own children, the children of friends, and the easy children. I also remember when I would have preferred it if my children would disappear. I remember when I preferred to poke my eyes out rather than go to work. And when I consider tomorrow, I can safely assume that I will battle preference versus responsibility all day long. It has been a lifelong pattern. I can *easily* remember this—I simply *can't* forget.

What is difficult to remember, and often forgotten, is the way in which Christ acted and interacts toward me. I understand the difficulty of setting preferences aside very well, but in a Christ-like way I cannot justify or rationalize any oversight activities wherein my personal preferences ought to be considered. If Christ *had* a preference it might have been to remain with the Godhead; to forgo thirty-some years among fallen beings with the accompanying consequences; and today He might prefer not to deal with my daily infirmities, constantly making intercession on my behalf. But I don't believe He had or considered personal preference. His work for His people was His *only* preference.

Prejudice. Fear drives conclusions about what will happen *if,* and it causes the outcome to be pre-managed before the results of the presumed *if,* come out. This problem drives more students away from Christ *alone* than it does attract them to Him; this can be seen both with students that have been successfully manipulated to avoid pre-judgment by purposefully living the religious group norm; and with those rejecting the emotional manipulation of the religious group norm, purposefully acting out the self-fulfilling prophecy of the pre-judgment. Excuse my vulgarity in seeking to make an important point about children: they are the best bull-shit detectors in the world. They will sense and react to prejudice, either as posers or as oppositional.

Let me give a simple example of such prejudice. I received a phone call from a staff member in connection with a student that was known through the grapevine of "good" kids to have used marijuana at some time in the past, and also was known to have a clinical diagnosis that requires medication. The "good" kids talk a lot about the marijuana to staff members and staff members eat it up as evidence of the goodness of the good. The premise of the telephone call was to seek a course of action in which the stated pre-judgment was that the student was on illegal drugs. The student was stumbling, the speech was slurred, and he seemed to go in and out of consciousness. Accompanying the pre-judgment was an implicit demand to me for swift, decisive and definitive action with the words, "we (the school) need to be 'done' with this student."

Due to the urgency of the physical symptoms I passed over the prejudice and the implicit demand and asked, "what would we do if Clyde (one of the "good" students) exhibited these physical symptoms?" The immediate answer, "call his parents and tell them that something is *seriously* wrong with Clyde." I replied, "ok, do that. And if you cannot reach them or they cannot come immediately, I authorize ambulatory transport to the nearest emergency room and the child must be accompanied by a staff member until a parent arrives. Hang up and do it now without acting as if you are a diagnostician."

Much later that day I phoned the parent of this student to see how he was doing. The child and parent had just recently arrived home from the emergency room and from a visit to the child's doctor. The child had been given a new medication the previous day, a necessity for the diagnosed illness and that had caused an allergic reaction. By the time the parent had picked the child up, the student had begun violent vomiting.

How does pre-judgment cloud our judgment of appropriate actions? *If* the child had been illegal-drug over-dosing would *agapao* dictate some different response? Why would time be taken to discuss the enrollment status of a child believed to be in danger from drug overdose? And what would be the devastating impact had we responded based on pre-judgment rather than on what was actually happening at the time—while waiting for the outcome to come out?

Conclusion

Perhaps the contemporary Christian community has lost a sense of awe regarding the impossible enormity of oversight in the Christian school. Such a position is not merely to educate and also have the freedom to talk about Jesus. It is not to educate and act as an evangelist. It is not to be nicer than non-Christian educators. It is not to educate while providing a well-behaved role model of what to do or how to live. It is not to manage or manipulate behavior. And it is not *only* to teach all content through the lens of a Biblical world and life view. A believing educator is prepared, passionate, and purposeful in living as an organic representation of Jesus Christ in learning relationships that have as their *only* foundation *agapao*—the love without conditions.

The commitment to represent *selfless love* ensures that the self-aware overseer will walk a *via dolorosa*, even if only as a result of the inner turmoil created by a sincere desire to emulate Christ; relationships that present a wide variety of human failure; and under the weight of the curse. The job of a Christian educator *is* possible when resting in Christ *alone*, and also rewarding and exhilarating. But it is not for the faint of heart. A school where overseers are called and equipped to let go of fear in *agapao* is filled with a spirit of liberty—and there is no place on earth where learning is deeper or broader—whether for purposes of this life or the next, and regardless of the height of the academic scores as evidenced by data.

It is the job of overseer to recognize and reduce the influence of *eros, phileo, and storge* in the learning environment to ensure that *agapao* is dominant. In an earlier chapter I wrote that openly oppositional people grow up and/or appear within the community of faith. This is *especially and most insidiously* true with the "hidden" opposition of professed Christians who have been taught that their outward group norm is synonymous with spirituality—and whose other loves are openly tolerated while remaining unchallenged. It's often called things like "control freak," or "too nice," or "rule follower" and worn like a badge of honor. Well everyone has issues—but I pray that overseers will not allow these issues to affect children and their view of Christ without a challenge just because the exterior is lookin' good and not a personal bother to the overseer.

If the overseers do not learn to *parissos* (abundantly exceed), they will continue and grow even more as the arbiters of group norm, failing to force the hidden darkness into the open light of Christ. And the darkness of these times will deepen to the degree that focus is directed toward the interpretation of the *appearance* of things, rather than the *underlying* things.

> "Jesus answered them saying, "When it is evening, you say it will be nice weather tomorrow because the sky is red. And in the morning you say, it will be storming today because the sky is red and threatening. O you hypocrites, you know how to interpret the *appearance of things*, but you cannot interpret *underlying things*. (Matthew 16:2-3, paraphrase mine)

18

Free and Fearless Confidence

> "Since we have this hope (Christ alone), we use much free and fearless confidence in speech (*parrhesia,* also translated "great plainness of speech"), because where the spirit of the Lord is, there is liberty. Since we have this command of God to proclaim and promote (*diakonia,* also translated "ministry"), and since we have received mercy, we do not become weary . . . but clearly set forth the execution of God's purposes in Jesus Christ (*aletheia,* also translated 'truth'). We stand firm, leaving it to each person's conscience in the presence of the one true God. If our good news is hidden, it is hidden to those who are lost."
> (2 Corinthians 3:12, 17 and 4:1–3, paraphrase mine)

The Bible texts paraphrased above express the heart of Paul's methodology as a preacher, that of free and fearless confidence in speech. Is there a reason this modus operandi would not apply when executing the ministry of teaching in the Christian school? Provided, of course, that one believes himself or herself to be operating based on the command of God to proclaim and promote (*diakonia*)—in this case through education, the teaching of Christ in content and process (*aletheia*).

Not all Christian educators have the gift or organizational position to speak publicly, but it cannot be argued that they *should not* be concerned with the continual development of free and fearless confidence in expressing the *diahonia aletheia* (ministry of truth) in words, within the context of individual responsibilities. *Are* Christian educators able to articulate, in all areas of application within the school, free and fearless communication about what it means to teach Christ in content and process? Phrasing the question another way, Do they know the *truth* enough to *wield it* in the educational setting, so that when it comes to *grace* they know when, or when not, to *yield*?

If teaching Christ in content and process is the vision at the apex of a hierarchy, mission aspirations; general goals; and precise, detailed objectives for the work will all follow in theological and philosophical harmony with that vision. Since "teaching Christ in content and process" contains in itself non-negotiable propositions, it follows that *some* missions, goals, and objectives will be opposed to, and therefore excluded from, consideration under this vision. Consequently, when teachers of this particular vision (truth) understand the relationship between the apex and all of the lesser categories of activity within a solid biblical framework, they will be equipped to speak with unhindered confidence. Using Paul's methodology the ministry of preaching and teaching is continually strengthened, while inhibited, timid communication chokes a spirit of liberty from the lungs of an organization.

The primary point of this chapter is to encourage teachers and administrators to pursue communication that is freely and fearlessly confident, in a variety of means and contexts, *in truth*. There is no factor more integral to the maintenance of a dominant spirit of liberty than the confident, non-negotiable, and gracious communication of that one primary vision (teaching Christ in content and process) than that of knowing and speaking its connection to all facets of the school community.

To illustrate that point I will provide an example. I hope it will go without saying that there are many ways and situations in which this methodology of Paul could and should be applied. In this case, a meeting had been arranged in response to alarming and widely disseminated allegations concerning a particular classroom. A few parents had drawn up and communicated their own definitive conclusions, presenting them as fact. (Other, less objective terms to fit the context might be *malice*, *slander*, or *gossip*). These conclusions reached the teacher and myself as statements about the inappropriate behavior of particular students as enrollees in the school; the inability of the teacher (and aide) to manage the classroom; and administrative failure in discipline. The misinformation had been spread widely, making it impossible to address discretely, on a one-on-one basis. The source, though suspected, was not known.

I chose for the purpose of the meeting to prepare a speech, to be followed up with questions and discussion. After an opening prayer I delivered (informally, without notes) the portion of the speech to follow; the concepts were illustrated in both outline and pictorial format on a whiteboard.

"Thanks for coming tonight. Let me begin by clarifying why we're here. Actually, there are different levels to why we're here. First, we're *here in this room tonight* because the teacher and I want to speak *openly in the school* about what has already been talked about *out of school* without our presence. Since "out of school" conversations pertain only to the information that can be passed along by children, and the parties to the conversation are not themselves *in the school* during the day, we felt that each parent would want the teacher and me, who *are* here all day, every day, to address the concerns with you.

"A second and deeper reason the teacher and I are here *every day, all day* is to teach Christ in *content* and *process*. To teach Christ in *content* means that we teach everything from a biblical world-and-life view, and to teach Christ in *process* means that we act and interact with everyone in the way in which Christ has acted and interacted with us. On that basis there are some other goals we *don't* have in this school—because they are mutually exclusive from, and even diametrically opposed to, teaching Christ *only* in content and process. We're okay without those other goals, but we want to be honest about this so that every parent will be able to make choices about whether they want a *Christ-centered* education for their children. In a minute I'll share three of the goals *we cannot have*.

"But first I need to remind you of one other thing concerning the teacher and myself. We are exactly like your children—conceived and born in sin. Because we know that about ourselves we listen carefully to, and consider, every concern that is communicated to us—whether from a parent or a child or a colleague—in order to consider how we might grow to be more and more like Jesus. So we're happy for this opportunity to address your concerns openly and share what is actually happening and actually being done in this classroom. After doing that we'll answer any questions or address any additional concerns you may have.

"First of all, teaching Christ in content and process and *trying to remove all barriers from a child's path* are mutually exclusive—absolutely incompatible—as goals. That means we don't hover over every child and pay extremely close attention to experiences and problems between peers, seeking to manipulate circumstances or swoop in to remove every challenge. The good news is that we do pay very close attention to every child as a one-of-a-kind, exquisite creation of Almighty God, seeking to guide each one to navigate their own unique interactions in a way that honors God and serves others. Exceptions are when the interactions threaten emotional or physical safety or academic progress—in which case we swoop in faster than you can imagine!

"The content that excludes that goal is that God is sovereign (and we are not), and the process that demonstrates this is surrender to His control (rather than exerting our own control)—this teaches the child to walk with God in Christ. Think about what life would be like for the adult whose childhood school had spent its time avoiding *developmentally appropriate* opportunities for children to problem solve. In practical terms, significantly diminished capacity for independence and regulation of one's behavior would result from such avoidance. I hope it is comforting for you to know that your child's teacher is working to know your child well enough to guide them toward the independence and self-regulation of walking with God, while guarding their emotional and physical safety and academic progress.

"Second, teaching Christ in content and process and *protecting 'good' children from 'bad' children* are, again, diametrically opposed. When people remark that they have spent a considerable amount on private schooling for this second purpose, I inform them that 'no amount of money will do that and no one in the world can promise that, nor should any human being have that as an objective.' To teach Christ in content is to teach that 'all have sinned and fallen short of the glory of God' and are in need of a Savior. In process that means that the classroom teacher enters relationships with individual students in order to point them to Christ as their highest good.

"There are no 'good' or 'bad' children at this school. There are, however, as many variations on behavioral, physical, mental, emotional, academic, and spiritual needs as there are students, and all of these are the results of sin, the fall, and the curse. Because of this we cannot eliminate a 'bad' child to ensure that a 'good' child does not become 'bad,' though there are times when the unique needs of a child exceed our ability or resources to address. In such cases, and with great sorrow, we tell the parents of that child the truth regarding our inadequacy for meeting these needs and assist in any way possible to help find a more suitable placement.

"The vast majority of the time the teacher is able to meet the unique needs of every student in the class because the school has a careful process to figure this out *before* a child is enrolled. Even then, our motivation is not to keep out the 'bad' but to avoid putting a child in a difficult situation. Having said that, we are very concerned about behavior—because we love and desire the growth of each student in the classroom. All the teachers at this school use a well-defined framework called Progressive Discipleship, which we will explain in detail in a few minutes.

"Third, teaching Christ in content and process *while pushing any unique child to exceed what is appropriate for them* represent incompatible goals. The classroom teacher isn't particularly concerned about whether a given child goes to Harvard or becomes an NBA player, doctor, lucrative business owner, or any other idealized preconception. The classroom teacher is *very* concerned about the child's ability to fearlessly discover his or her unique strengths and weaknesses, so that learning and development as an individual, created in God's image and for His purpose, progresses throughout the years of schooling.

"*Ideation* is the process of forming an idea and then seeking to control all of the steps toward its actualization in the physical world. In the context of education this often shows up in the attempts of parents to manage or manipulate all stages and conditions of a child's experience in an effort to produce the actualization of the *parent's* ideal for what the child should become. Aside from the fact that this approach is contrary to teaching Christ in content and process, it is extremely sad to watch a child become shackled to the ideation of an adult; he or she is unable to form an appropriate sense of identity and lives without the freedom to explore his or her own possibilities.

"In terms of content, we teach that God has a unique design and purpose for each child. Consequently, our process cannot prohibit a child from exploring and embracing himself or herself as an individual, while preparing them to fill the role and place God has designed for them, academically, socially, emotionally, and spiritually. *Any* exceptions to that exploration have to do with the Word and law of *God*. The classroom environment is designed to allow for exploration within an orderly framework—with God's law and Word as central and absolute and with a written curriculum designed to ensure vertical and progressive presentation of content, skills, and practices, based on external and objective standards. The school environment is designed to allow for extracurricular opportunities for the same purpose: self-discovery and varied learning. The teachers are trained to modify classroom content, as objectively indicated by the needs of the individual child, but not in response to the ideation of an adult regarding the child's future life." (*End of example.*)

The speech continued with an explanation and example of Progressive Discipleship, and the meeting ended with dialogue around questions and concerns. The outcomes were positive, as far as it was possible to discern. Many parents expressed thanks and pleasant surprise that the teacher and I were "so knowledgeable." Even if a particular family had opted to withdraw from the school based on *the truth contained in this speech*, we would have considered the outcome positive in terms of *truth* as a divider, while we were graciously *yielding*.

When one understands exactly *what* they are doing, and *why* they are doing it, they are enabled to speak about the issues without inhibition. When the *what* and *why* are related to a vision of teaching Christ in content and process, and the walk matches the talk, the education will excel (in the most excellent way of 1 Corinthians 12:31) in comparison to any other educational experience anywhere in the world.

The problem for us as Christian educators, as I have articulated already in many ways, is not that we lack "best practice" in education. The problem is that we lack the spiritual vision to teach Christ *alone* in content and process; that spiritual problem has led to poor educational practice. Scrambling to "catch up" to best practice is never the answer. The *best* practice is in fact simply to practice what we preach and teach. As Christ enjoined His followers, "*You* seek the kingdom *first*, and *then* all these other things will be added to you" (Matthew 6:33, emphasis mine).

I said something else in the meeting. While tears were forming rivulets down my cheeks, I stated passionately, "If your child gets one or two teachers in their entire lifetime like the teacher they have right now, you should fall to your knees and thank almighty God, because *this one* is a master teacher emulating *the* Master Teacher, Jesus Christ—deeply knowing and deeply loving your child. *That* experience will do infinitely more that is good for children than any naughty, annoying child will *ever* do that is 'bad' for them."

I said that because I meant it, because it's true, and because I have seen the power of this dynamic in so many lives. But I also say it here, in the context of this book, as a reminder for Christian school overseers of teacher underlings to make sure that every teacher in the Christian school is a master teacher, or growing demonstrably toward becoming one. Stated candidly, they must grow or they must go. By "master teacher" I mean clearly and consistently representative of Christ, as well as skilled in the art of teaching and learning from within a solidly biblical framework.

Permit me to share a few examples of children whose psyches have been imprisoned. These jail cells can swing open only through unfettered confidence in speaking truth. Here again, the jailers of these children might opt to walk away from truth, along with the shackled child; if this is indeed the case, so be it. The pain of watching people walk away from truth is far outweighed by the joy of seeing someone else freed by it. In case a reader would conclude that open admissions is the cause of the problems suggested by the illustrations, note that all of the examples in this chapter (and some of the others in the book) are drawn from the lives of professed Christians who regularly attend church.

Poop Smearing—An upper elementary student is outwardly well behaved, not because he is obedient but because he is deathly afraid of anything that might precipitate an interaction between his teacher and his parents. On the rare occasions when such interaction has been necessary, the teachers were verbally bullied in return for their trouble. The boy appears to live in a hellish prison; an only child, he is plagued in the extreme by the hovering, incessant presence of his angry, unhappy parents, whose sole aim in life appears to be to fix all the failure and sorrow of their own lives by re-creating the child in the image of what they are not.

This much is fairly obvious through observation, but the depth of this boy's pain was most poignantly revealed when it was determined that he was regularly smearing feces in the bathroom stall. Imagine the extremities of experience that necessitate the smearing of feces at school. Imagine if that were the only way one could exercise some control in their own life; or experience a sense of ownership over their own actions; or express anger, frustration, helplessness, or powerlessness. *Was I afraid to have that conversation?* Absolutely!

Why did God bring this young man to a Christian school? I only know that He *did.* During and immediately following the poop-smearing conversation I felt as though I had done battle with evil spirits. In Proverbs 18:10 Solomon points out that "the name of the LORD is a strong tower; the righteous runs into it and is safe" (NASB). We will continue to *yield ourselves in grace* so that we can *wield the truth* to this young man and to his parents as long as the Lord allows. At any time they could easily cross boundaries we won't negotiate, or walk away because they are repelled by the truth. Our prayer is that all three might be freed from their prison.

Really!?*—A little boy presents as a model of typical early elementary behavior and academic progress. Nothing out of the ordinary has been noted at school before or after the exchange between his mother and his teacher. The mother requested a meeting with the teacher to express two concerns, the first that the child was exhibiting bad behavior *at home* and that, according to Mom, it could only be attributed to the influence of bad children *at school* from whom the teacher was not protecting him.

The second concern was that the teacher did not send home enough homework: "If you (the teacher) don't assign the work, it's difficult for me (the mother) to motivate him to do the 40 minutes of homework per night that *I* require." I can only respond (here in the book) with "*Really!*?*" Pause. "I find it difficult to imagine where the behavioral problem *at home* is coming from." Please *do* read heavy sarcasm into the previous sentence.

(The reader might also note that I experience the same struggles with being graciously unapologetic as anyone else might. Probably more. According to God's unique design in me I am able to speak the truth easily, and even unapologetically; to do so with appropriate grace is much more of a challenge. This is sad because when I speak the truth without grace my sin nature speaks more loudly than my words of truth, and I obscure a vision of Christ *alone* from shining. Many a time I find myself impelled to return—either to God, or people, or to both—to repent and turn again from my old self toward Christ *alone*. If you've read this far I'm sure you'll have no trouble imagining this.)

But thankfully, the teacher spoke to the mom with free and fearless confidence in the ministry of truth, while graciously setting aside the implied accusations against herself. Who knows what the ultimate outcome may be? One of the bittersweet realities of teaching Christ in content and process is that one rarely foresees the long-term effects of our *diahonia aletheia*.

"My Princess"—Finally, I recall the girl who transferred to a school where I was working when she was entering the seventh grade. This was the fifth school she had attended; the reason given for the frequent moves was that "none of those schools were good enough for my princess." During the course of the conversation the father variously referred to his daughter as his "pride and joy" and "his world" and expressed that "if she were hurt or saddened I would die."

Despite the implied flattery concerning my school, I felt compelled to speak some truth into that first conversation: "I *can't* guarantee this school will be a castle for your princess. I *can* guarantee that this school is filled with sinners. Are you sure you're going to be comfortable with your daughter's attendance here?" He assured me that he would. I feared that he was mistaken but set those fears aside. Exactly as I had expected, it became necessary to spend a good deal of time speaking truth, both to him and to his daughter. Needless to say, his underlying reason for the frequent school changes was *not* that the schools were inadequate for his princess—nor had I ever suspected that it was.

This poor girl was acting out, a by-product of trying to carry the responsibility for her father's precarious state of emotional health. Emotional incest has devastating consequences, and by the middle of the eighth grade this young lady was self-destructively looking for love in all the wrong places—desperately seeking the love of her father *toward* her rather than his worship of himself *through* her. One day after school she and a boy were found in an empty room after school; she was performing oral sex.

This incident, horrible as it was, allowed for the free and fearless confidence of *diahonia aletheia*. This was a rare case of my being enabled to witness the truth exercising immediate power—opening the eyes of the father sufficiently to transform his understanding of himself and his responsibilities with regard to his daughter. Occasionally still he sends a message of thanks. The power of truth drove him to counseling, to his knees, and to the Father in heaven. It is the *Truth* (the Word)—not you or me—that has power. Are Christian educators equipping themselves through ongoing study to *speak it*?

The chart below might be helpful as a basis for overseer/underling relationships or partnerships with parents. Keep in mind that to develop free and fearless confidence in *diahonia aletheia* requires one to act as a representative of Christ alone in content and process, discovering and setting aside personal motivations that are rooted in fear. Interactions that are so rooted grow and bloom into the weed of control—by contrast, in love into the flower of liberty.

Love	Fear
. . . prepares for a covenant life in the world	. . . requires moral life of the world
. . . pursues long-term character development	. . . satisfied with short-term compliance
. . . motivates with love	. . . motivates with fear
. . . establishes thoughtful order	. . . enforces uniform control
. . . digs for the heart of the issue	. . . manages external elements of the issue

Free and fearless confidence in speaking *diahonia aletheia* is the apex of all learning outcomes in Christian education. This happens when a student is captivated by a vision of Christ alone through all content, so that Christ is found to be meeting the deepest need and life begins in a process of surrendering to His obedience, the highest good. Are Christian educators driving students to that apex by modeling it in word and deed? To be graciously unapologetic is to be free and fearless in confidence, while walking and talking the ministry of truth.

The majority of families in the Christian school are not operating in the extremes of the examples I use, although no given family or child has a lesser need of free and fearless confidence in truth than any other. But the additional point here, at the close of this chapter, is that the world is crumbling, and that the truly Christian church and school are not escaping the fallout. Shouldn't every knowledgeable reader of the Bible and of history suspect that the incidence of the extremes will increase? Didn't this happen in the approach to the first coming of Jesus? This being the case, is the duty of Christian educators to self-protect? The testimony of Paul and the other apostles demands that a believer put on the full armor of God (Ephesians 6) and live in a confident and ready stance.

> "Now to him who is able to keep you from stumbling and to present you blameless before the presence of his glory with great joy, to the only God, our Savior, through Jesus Christ our Lord, be glory, majesty, dominion, and authority, before all time and now and forever. Amen." (Jude 1:24–25, ESV)

19

Chazown Parats

"Now the boy Samuel was ministering to the LORD in the presence of Eli. And the word of the LORD was rare in those days; there was no frequent (*parats*, bursting out) vision (*chazown*, divine communication). (1 Samuel 3:1, ESV)

Why write a book about spiritual renewal in Christian education and say nothing about the art of teaching or of its effectiveness with learners? First, because copious excellent pedagogical resources are readily available. And second, because well-targeted education doesn't prohibit the kings and kingdoms of the earth from cyclical rising and falling—at the present time, most would agree, there is more apparent falling than rising. (This is so despite the widely circulated claims by Christian churches and schools that "restoration," "transformation," and "impact" will result from their work in the earth—not primarily in terms of the salvation of souls but in the earth itself.)

The reason this book only minimally addresses the teaching and learning functions is that "the word of the LORD is rare in *these* days" too; therefore it will not ultimately matter *which* pedagogical resources are chosen and implemented. If God's "divine communication" does not "'burst out" among the people of God, Christian education will be guilty of contributing to its own fall, but also to the fall of kings and kingdoms based on the absence of vision.

Chazown parats (vision bursting out)—if by God's design—will either stop the falling or activate the next rising, whether of another earthly kingdom or of His consummated kingdom.

The world has always taken counsel against God's anointed, throwing off His restraints, and it will continue to do so until the Lord returns—continually raging and imagining vain things (Psalm 2:1–3). Sadly, professed Christians seem also to have cast off the restraint of their One legitimate vision, Jesus Christ. "Whoever is not with me is against me, and whoever does not gather with me scatters," Jesus declared (Matthew 12:30, ESV). Have *professed Christ followers* taken counsel against the Lord, and against His anointed One (Psalm 2:2)—if not by outward denial then by sad neglect? Are *they* among those who are raging (frantic work) and vain in their imaginations of "Christ *and* something else" (Psalm 2:1)?

> "Long ago, at many times and in many ways, God spoke to our fathers by the prophets, but in these last days he has spoken (*laleo*, declared His mind and disclosed His thoughts) to us by his Son (*Huios*), whom he appointed the heir of all things, through whom also he created the world." (Hebrews 1:1–2, ESV)

God's plan has been well and fully communicated—in the past in many ways and at various times, as well as in the present through His Son. *Huios* means (minimally) "Christ, fully God and fully man, acting in glorious concert with the Trinity, as Son of the Father and co-laborer with the Spirit, in the realization of a redemptive plan so that those whom the Father has given Him will enjoy the fellowship of the godhead and glorify Him forever in the new heavens and earth—and returning a second time to judge all humankind and fully restore all things to Himself" (definition mine).

The *Huios* is also called Word (*logos*) in John 1:1. The Son *is* the full embodiment in flesh of all divine communication. Jesus Christ *is* the *chazown*, the vision. And spiritual renewal is a result of *chazown* that is *parats*. This bursting out of vision is needed *before* (in order of importance and placement) enrollment, financial resources, pedagogies—and yes, even above and beyond whatever is believed to provide sustainability.

Contemporary vision (or highest objective) statements in Christian schools contain presumed and particular outcomes of the schools' work—in both obvious and subtle ways—as though these visions contain new information subject to private interpretation. Sadly, such vision within Christian organizations is pandemic wishful thinking, disobedient to the command, and often in direct conflict to what has already been communicated in the Word. And yet the fruit of the promise is "named and claimed" in return for these grandiose efforts undertaken *for* Christ.

Christ is increasingly relegated to the lower regions of hierarchy, while particular organizational visions that predict an inspirational outcome manipulate emotions, eliciting increased involvement and taking a position at the uppermost pinnacle of hierarchy—this is, I would posit, the very definition of unequivocally having a form of godliness while denying the power thereof (2 Timothy 3:5). Teach (or preach) Christ, if you will, to people suffering from any of the wide range of the consequences of human corruption, in grace and truth, with any resources available, and using any object lesson lawful. But *start* with a vision of Christ *alone*.

A particular Christian school articulates in its vision statement that "every student (will be) prepared to impact the world for Jesus Christ" and that "an [*insert school name*] education transforms the heart as well as the mind." There are at least three pieces of new information stated or presumed (superimposed upon and in conflict with what has been revealed in Christ) in the excerpts from this school's vision statement: First, that all students of this school will impact the world. Second, that Jesus Christ lacks something and that these students can provide it *for* Him with their impact. And third, that "this school" has the power to transform the heart and mind of, minimally, these students. Christ himself did not make such presumptuous claims; instead He declared that "those that *the Father gives to me* will come to me" (John 6:37, ESV, emphasis mine).

I find it necessary to pause here to make two points. First, of the numerous school leaders who have engaged in dialogue with me around vision statements, all but one have argued "But that's not what we *mean*" when I've suggested what I have in the example above. Just as one might respond to a student who retorts "That's not what I *meant*" after having pronounced the *f*-word in school, one might say to these school leaders, "It isn't what you *mean* that concerns me—it's what you *said*. Say what you mean, and mean what you say." The words we choose have consequences, not to mention that they flow from the heart. Vulgarity might indeed be preferable to the profanity of stating, or even suggesting, that a Christian school has the power to accomplish what only God can do without mentioning Him—whether or not they *mean* it that way. The second point: I picked one particular school as an example. *Every* school I've encountered, *including the one where I lead*, has work to do in the area of understanding "vision" from a biblical perspective. As do I.

Another Christian school communicates its vision in this way: "Our grand plan (highest objective, vision) remains the same: growing exceptional and distinctive opportunities for students, building and equipping a world-class Christian school faculty and staff, and developing lasting enhancements within our finances, facilities, and school community." These are (mostly) legitimate strategic goals—but vision? I say "mostly" because I can't help but wonder whether "world-class" and "Christian" are oxymoronic. Certainly worth exploring if the two are coupled in the vision statement of a *Christian* school.

Christian schools have learned well this "vision lesson" from Christian churches. In a popular resource titled *Church Relevance*, where over one hundred thousand subscribers find help to make their churches relevant (in itself a sign of alarming spiritual illness), "vision" is defined as follows. "Vision Statement (Desired End-State): a one-sentence statement describing the clear and inspirational long-term desired change resulting from an organization or program's work."

Note three points in connection with this definition. First, the "desired end state" is nothing more than wishful thinking—unless the particular end-state is revealed in Scripture. Second, the "desired change" is a result of the organization or program's work. And third, the desired end-state, or vision, must be inspirational. Is "the full embodiment of divine communication, in flesh" not inspirational enough for Christian churches and schools? Is the emphasis on inspiration and cultural relevance a strategy to attract participants to be involved in reaching the "desired end state"?

What if Christian schools were instead to impose upon themselves the restraint of the one obedient vision that addresses all the physical and spiritual aspects of learning? If to teach is the command, Christ *alone* is the vision, and application to content and process indeed covers all aspects of learning, then the one obedient vision can only be to teach Christ *alone* in content and process. (For the church, "teach" could be replaced with "preach.") Plenty of latitude flows from that vision for setting strategic goals and crafting operating objectives within the context of God's placement of a particular school. I don't know about relevance, but if Christian education were driven by this one obedient vision, that would be *chazown parats*.

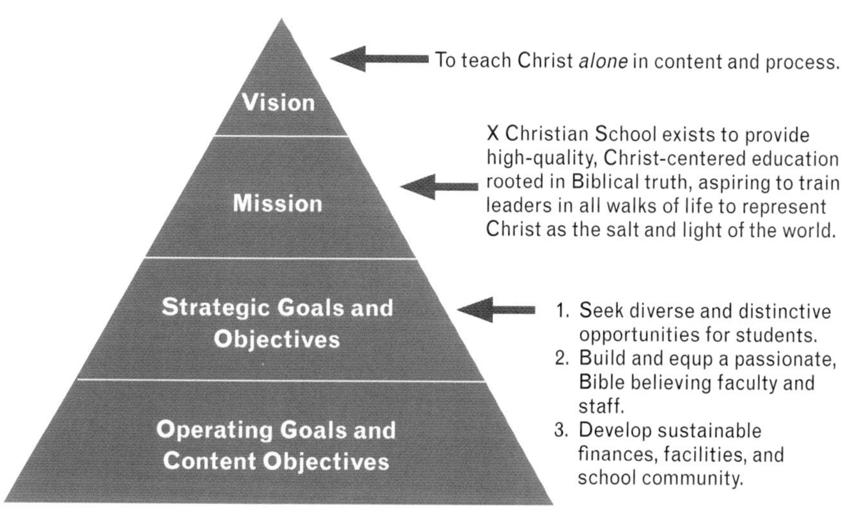

I'm quite aware that the vision I'm suggesting isn't very, well, sexy, or apparently relevant, but from a biblical standpoint Christian schools exist for no other reason than to teach Christ, the full embodiment in flesh of all divine communication. Is it the case that other strategic and operational activities will flow *out of* that vision? Yes, but my contention is that if teaching Christ *alone* can't get the subordinate strategic or operational job done, it's just possible that the particular subordinate job isn't worth doing.

A vision to teach Christ *alone* in content and process (obedient input) results in passionate consistency in grace and non-negotiable accountability to truth (promised output). Naturally that will impact the entire school community, drawing many to Him while repelling others. And if by God's design, this vision will also impact strategic goals and operating objectives with favorable results. Either way, true obedience is to let go of the need to seek control of the outcome for results that are perceived (by humans) to be favorable.

That which flows from a vision of Christ (restrained obedience) springs from His power and produces the outcome of God's predetermined will. That which flows, on the other hand, from any humanly manufactured vision (casting off the restraint of Christ's obedience) can rely upon only the human force contained in the participants—which though in some cases, where there are plentiful financial resources, constitutes organizational strength can never equate to spiritual strength. Human force will, ultimately, also result in God's predetermined will, as in fact everything does. But I do not believe any Christian educator desires *that* particular outcome.

> "Where there is no prophetic vision (*chazown*, divine communication), the people (`*am*, kindred, nation, people) cast off restraint (*para`*, are loosed from restraints): but blessed is he who keeps the law (*towrah*, God's full instruction)." (Proverbs 29:18, ESV)

There are two critical principles pertaining to the vision in this verse that, if recognized at all, are widely ignored. To demonstrate its impact *without taking into account these critical principles*, I'll rephrase it in a way that reflects the manner in which the verse is most often (incorrectly) construed: Where there is no vision, the land in which I live will be wild and unruly and immoral: but I keep the law and am blessed because I'm a Christian, so the inspirational idea that is most emotionally moving to me *must and will be* the vision *du jour*, which will "save" the land I love!

The first critical principle is that Christ alone *is* the *chazown*. This verse does not intend a particular, targeted vision being newly communicated as an individual or organizational desired –end state—certainly not now that God has communicated through *Huios* (Hebrews 1:1–3). This much has been discussed earlier in the chapter. But further, the verse refers to the blessed one as "he who keeps God's full instruction." This can only and ultimately refer to Christ, although it applies by extension to those who are *in* Christ—but only in the sense that they are recipients of all the blessings that belong to Him. In the resounding words of Paul, "Blessed be the God and Father of our Lord Jesus Christ, who has blessed us in Christ with every spiritual blessing in the heavenly places" (Ephesians 1:3, ESV).

The second critical principle is that the people (*`am*) who cast off the restraint are *first* the people of God. By implication and consequence, this casting off also has an impact on the lands in which the believers reside—because they are representatives of the light of Christ. When believers are not restrained by the *chazown*, their light is covered and hence concealed (Matthew 5:14–16). Proverbs 29:18 is *first* a prophetic word regarding what will happen when believers lack a vision of Christ: they will cast off the restraint of Christ's obedience. Ultimately, this lack of vision will bring about their spiritual death and then also plunge the land in which they live into an equally unrestrained spiritual darkness.

I'm suggesting that we bind Christian education, through its leaders, to the one legitimate vision for a Christian (Christ) school (to teach). We'll have to let go of any particular wishful ideas about the outcome of the work. A relief, right? After that, all that needs doing is to work strategically and operationally to apply the grace and truth of Christ to all teaching and learning in each unique context. To state this more plainly, when Christ is taught as Lord people will act as though they believe it. God will make Himself responsible for all of the consequences into which obedience leads.

At the present time believers without *chazown parats* are in imminent danger of being swept away by a tidal wave. And how will the children we teach (all of whom are sojourners, in the spiritual sense of the word) stand against the wave if we have not constrained them to a singular vision of Christ *alone*? How indeed will *we* stand, having loosed ourselves from His restraint? The believer has only One restraint: the obedience of Christ. Everything *else*—based on the very premise and reality of that restraint—is liberty.

If Christian education as a whole crumbles (spiritually, physically, or both), it will be because the restraint of Christ has been cast off, so that the *chazown parats* is missing. If faith is scarce on the earth it will be for the same reason. If the nation crumbles and is plunged into spiritual darkness, there will be none to blame but those who know *about* Christ but have cast off His restraint, no longer knowing *Him* and therefore lacking *chazown parats*. Clinging to the contemporary form of Christian school "vision" is like rushing into a burning building, yelling "Blow out the fire with your breath; don't bother calling the fire department!" It doesn't matter how inspiring this sounds or how many people follow into the fire: it has a form of heroism while denying the power of water.

After years of Israel's casting off the restraints of God's covenant and law, King Josiah renovated the temple. In the process the long-ago-recorded law and covenant were discovered and read to him. Upon hearing the convicting words he tore his clothes in repentance. There is much to learn from the full account of King Josiah, but in this connection it is interesting to note that he did not only insist upon Israel's living differently but also cast down all the "high places"' (2 Kings 22–23). Is this what Paul intends for New Testament believers when he refers to "casting down all imaginations that raise themselves against the knowledge of God and the obedience of Christ" (1 Corinthians 10:5)? Should the situation be any different when contemporary visions align themselves against the obedience of Christ?

Is it enough to move *toward* this One vision? *Chazown Parats*: a vivid, sublime mental image of the glorious fullness of Christ that continually and fearlessly grows and reaches for His likeness, both in all the details of life (content) and in all ways of being (process). To maintain this beatific vision through devotion to Christ is not only obedience in *agapao* but bursts out of believers in His graciously unapologetic way (through us by Him, not by us for Him) to the world around as a beacon light on a hill, piercing the darkness all around it as it revolves. *Chazown parats* cannot fail because it is powered by *Huios*, whom God appointed the heir of all things and through whom He created the world. What "high imaginations" are in need of casting down so that Christ *alone* might be lifted up as vision?

How about beginning with casting down the idea that Jesus Christ is sitting around heaven like an impotent ruler, waiting for people to do "the work" of saving, either of souls or from the ills of the world, wringing His hands because we aren't doing enough *for Him*. Jesus Christ as the King of kings and Lord of lords is completely cognizant of all that is happening, and why. He needs nothing from any of us and will accomplish His own purposes in and through anything He wants. He demands from us obedience in love, not our effort to earn.

And God the Father is neither shocked nor saddened that the world is filled with sin and corruption—these come as no surprise to Him. He knows exactly how sin entered the world and why He cursed the earth. It was He who poured all His wrath upon Jesus, so that some might escape the curse. So when believers turn away from a vision of Christ *alone*, the One on whom the Father's wrath was poured, He gets ready to purge the threshing floor and cleanse it with fire—a far cry from sitting around pouting and manipulating us to "do the right thing." He demands that we find our all in Christ *alone*, not in Christ *and* something else.

Last, but certainly not least, the Holy Spirit enlivens souls that are spiritually dead—He is not waiting for the decisions of people in order to determine the recipients of salvation. He moves wherever and whomever He wills, changing hearts of stone to hearts of flesh. He causes the spiritually deaf to hear and the spiritually blind to see. He feeds hungry souls with the bread of life and causes thirsty souls to refresh themselves with living water. And He groans in intercession when God's people sin—more egregiously than our own immoral nation—in losing sight of Christ as vision, all the while chasing other gods.

The magnitude of the "visioning" that communicates that Christian churches and schools will fully or partially eliminate the effects of the fall is overwhelming. The Christian community is in so many words advertising its ability to solve global crises, restore the earth, end world hunger, stop addiction, transform the world, end sex-trafficking, and even save souls, etc., as visional outcomes of its work. And most of this "visioning" takes place in the context of organizations that *also* say Christ's kingdom is not of this world, rejecting the social gospel. Isn't that exactly what the Jews hated about Jesus? Because He wouldn't make the kingdom all about them? They were *so* attached to their visions of establishing their kingdom on "their earth" that they killed Him. Are we in effect killing Jesus with our focus on visions that indicate what we *wish*, instead of what we *know* in Christ *alone*, to be spiritual healing?

Anyone out there want renewal in their Christian school? Then drive your stake into the ground and put your own visions to death. Develop and maintain a vision of Christ and Christ alone, letting go of control of the outcome, and let all other activities flow from surrender to God's way without presuming God's intent. Incredible things will happen—that is for certain. Perhaps not the same "incredible things" that have been envisioned by human beings! God's kingdom and will (not of this earth and not of human devising) are certain to come *through* you *in* Him, but never *by* you *for* Him.

When praying "Thy kingdom come, Thy will be done," ask often which kingdom and will you are envisioning: His kingdom, with Christ on the throne, or the one being projected by your old self? His will and way, or the desired ends of your own vision? Jesus Christ *alone* is King; so surrender, or die.

> "In the year that King Uzziah died I saw the LORD sitting upon a throne, high and lifted up; and the train of his robe filled the temple. Above him stood the seraphim. Each had six wings: with two he covered his face, and with two he covered his feet, and with two he flew. And one called to another and said: Holy, holy, holy is the LORD of hosts; the whole earth is full of his glory!" (Isaiah 6:1–3, ESV)

> "Now may the God of peace who brought again from the dead our Lord Jesus, the great shepherd of the sheep, by the blood of the eternal covenant, equip you with everything good that you may do his will, working in us that which is pleasing in his sight, through Jesus Christ, to whom be glory forever and ever. Amen." (Hebrews 13:21–22, ESV)

20

The Lion and the Lamb

There are two reasons I withheld the story of Parkview Christian Academy (Parkview), the place of my current employ, until the end of the book. The first was to avoid a suggestion of cause and effect between content in the book and any particular outcomes at Parkview. Obedience in a Christian school is straightforward; it constitutes teaching Christ *alone* in content and process, elevating the Lord as the first priority in our heart and at the highest position of organizational hierarchy; while exercising the boldness to cast down all other imaginations.

Parkview was and remains obedient—but the outcome could have gone, and still could go, in either direction. This book isn't primarily meant for schools that appear to be dying organizationally (as was Parkview); it's intended to propose obedience as an antidote to spiritual illness, which I believe is plaguing Christian schools in various manifestations of organizational strength and weakness.

Second, throughout the book I pose challenging questions intended to provoke serious thought. A deep rootedness in the Word is the only appropriate basis for such inquiry. To incite conviction based upon an emotional reaction to an exciting story is tantamount to composing a school vision based upon wishful thinking, while seeking to inspire the emotions of stakeholders to get on board. When believers take the time and pains to arrive at truth, the result will invariably involve the emotions. But allowing emotions to lead deliberations, even if the outcome is temporally favorable, results in an impotent truth. Hence the reserving of this story for the end.

I convey it as a testimony to the power and presence of Christ, and as an expression of gratitude to God for the uncommon obedience of the believing people at Parkview, with a view to goading Christian educators toward the obedience of Christ—and not toward Parkview. Amid ostensibly hopeless circumstances the school board, along with a core of believing families, rejected the reasonable fear of extinction and chose instead the narrow and difficult way of obedience to Christ. They did this while cognizant that all indicators were suggesting cessation of Parkview's continuing identity as a school. They willingly and deliberately let go of the need to control or know the outcome. Allow me to begin with a little history.

The cornerstone of what was to become the Parkview main campus building was set in place in 1887 during the construction of the Yorkville School, which would accommodate students from kindergarten through the 12th grade in the city of Yorkville, Illinois, and the surrounding farm communities of Kendall County. For many years the Yorkville school district grew, and the original building served differing grade levels and community enterprises until 1991. On December 30, 1992, the building was purchased by the Parkview Foundation as the result of one family's interest in both Christian education and the preservation of a historic landmark.

A Parkview Foundation member and her friend (the founder and the first administrator, respectively, of the school) found themselves walking through the empty school building, which had fallen into disrepair, in 1996. At that time the friends had a conversation in which they discussed their shared hope that the historic school building might one day become home to a Christian school. As a result of that initial exchange Parkview Christian Academy opened in 1997 with eight students—with the communicated vision to provide families in Yorkville and the surrounding Kendall County a quality, Christ-centered education. One year at a time the Parkview school community reclaimed another classroom.

Parkview continues to this day as a lessee to Parkview Foundation in that same school building, currently in use as a preschool and elementary campus. This arrangement was made possible through the generosity of the Parkview Foundation, which lovingly maintains the beautiful building and grounds. I would be remiss in failing to note that the school was not always a lessee; for some time the building was used at no cost. Additionally, on several occasions the Parkview Foundation had invested in the school's survival through other means of support. The junior and senior high school campus of Parkview, also leased, is located a short distance away.

Before continuing with the story I feel compelled to allude to a dark side that cannot be printed in detail for at least three reasons: The details aren't conducive to description; there would be legal ramifications involved; and attempts to do so would distract the reader from the astonishing work of God in the story. Those enticing intimations notwithstanding, I am at liberty to state only that Parkview had been troubled by darkness for some time prior to its path crossing with my own. I mention this so that the glory of God may be demonstrated in contrast.

There is a sense in which all people live with internal darkness—even believers experience the darkness of the old sin-nature coexisting with their new, redeemed identity. But the darkness of which I speak here is different—unrestrained, as when the truth is exchanged for a lie (Romans 1:25), a wolf dons sheep's clothing (Matthew 7:15), or people have "walked in the way of Cain" (Jude 1:11). When *that* variety of darkness is present the times are ripe for fear, control, and confusion, the rejection of which is in itself evidence of God's triumphing *through* believers *in* Christ.

Prior to 2013 Parkview had experienced three periods of administrative leadership, each contributing pivotal resources God saw fit to store up as provision for survival in crisis. The first saw enrollment growth, strong community, monumental sacrifice, and a solid foundation in teachers possessing passion for both high-quality education and the teaching of Christ in content and process. That strong foundation included the founder and first administrator but when she retired, the same passion remained in the teaching staff. The second period saw a focus on the application of spiritual principles to relationship. And the third brought the implementation of technology to school management. By the fall of 2009 the school had expanded in two directions, with the formation of both high school and preschool programs.

From 1997–2013 the understanding and functionality of board governance seems to have grown steadily, though initially the school was functionally operated on an administrator-run basis. There are stories from this period of intermittent power struggles. But at the time of my arrival the board was functioning in strength—its focus on liberty, not control. And the consistent testimony of board members, families, and students has been that the teaching staff was an unwavering source of stability throughout all the years of the school.

> "The wicked flee when no one pursues, but the righteous are bold as a lion." (Proverbs 28:1, ESV)

At some point in the two years leading up to my meeting with Parkview as an interviewee, a family of considerable means and influence had entered into discussion with the school board about constructing and financing a state-of-the-art high school building to support and jump-start the development of the then fledgling high school. This exciting prospect remained in focus until the discussions stalled over three points: stipulations that the high school would have (1) an independent school board selected and led, in perpetuity, by the financing family; (2) a different school name; and (3) a different vision occupying the highest position of priority.

The board of Parkview took an unyielding *no* position on two points: the changing of vision from Christ-centered to *anything else at all* and the establishment of an alternate school board. Christ in Truth was discerned in the participants by the boldness of the stand that was taken—in this case "no"—reminiscent of the Lion of Judah; see Revelation 5:5. In response, the family pulled out early in 2013, taking with them the then current administrator, to move forward with their own plans. Parkview's doom was widely foretold, and the board was urged to throw in the towel and resign themselves to becoming a feeder school. To its credit Parkview proceeded in obedience, based upon *chazown parats*.

> "He was oppressed, and he was afflicted, yet he opened not his mouth: like a lamb that is led to the slaughter, and like a sheep that before its shearers is silent, so he opened not his mouth." (Isaiah 53:7, ESV)

The school community and the city of Yorkville had been very excited and motivated by the plans of a new high school building that had been widely advertised as would-be results of this particular families' proposed influx of money and influence. After the parting of ways some public scoffing commenced, and private attempts to cherry-pick students ensued. Christ's grace was evident during this time in a silence reminiscent of the Lamb of Isaiah 53:7 being led to slaughter. The board members of Parkview took care to maintain confidentiality and silent decorum while engaging in prayer. The school community as a whole was confused, hurt, and fearful. A few constituents discerned the happening truth, though many others became disgruntled and took sides, not knowing what to believe. I began work at Parkview as the fourth administrator at a time when the community was still suffering unmerited reproach. The pull-out took place in early spring of 2013, before the end of the school year. I arrived in August.

As an aside, I would suggest here that the work of spiritually sensitive school leaders and financial supporters around the world ought to be devoted to the Christian schools where Christ is found *in* the people leading—not where leadership is *doing* things *for* Christ. It is my notion that Christian education could be rapidly and deeply renewed in spirit were the efforts of zealous Christian educators and financial supporters devoted to discerning the difference—and willing to expend themselves on the former rather than the latter.

> "Remember this, O LORD, how the enemy scoffs, and a foolish people reviles your name. Do not deliver the soul of your dove to the wild beasts; do not forget the life of your poor forever." (Psalm 74:18–19, ESV)

In August 1st, 2013 the Parkview story and my own intersected formally in His-story. For me this was one of those precious life events when God's design in the juxtaposition of prayers, study, and events was visible and discernable. My prayers for an opportunity to apply and systematize a framework for spiritually renewed Christian education lined up perfectly with the external circumstances. So I took the job. (In truth, I did so also because my old sin-nature was riled up about the situation that had been described to me: "How *dare* they touch the apple of His eye?").

My first day at Parkview was defined by two disconcerting discoveries. While seated at the desk reviewing papers that had been stuffed into drawers, I uncovered the details of two effectively concealed financial difficulties. The first was a series of many months' notices regarding nonpayment of payroll tax over an extended period—complete with fines—and the second a sequence of legal letters on behalf of an association regarding notice of impending court proceedings due to nonpayment of a loan that had already been deferred for a three-year period. These looming financial calamities had gone undisclosed to the board during the previous administration, and the loan had apparently gone untracked and unrevealed during the previous two periods of administrative leadership. The notices and letters pertaining to both matters had been opened, unfolded, apparently read, and then stuffed into a drawer. Communication of these revelations constituted my first official items of business with the school board of Parkview.

If all other matters were in order, a Christian school might be able to absorb that kind of shock with minimal concern. But the situation at Parkview was already far from ideal. First, the previous two administrators, the second and third in the school's history, had each departed peremptorily during the early part of the second semester, within two years of each other, both under questionable circumstances. To make matters worse, queries of constituents could not be fully answered regarding either of these departures. In addition, both of these administrators had publicly and emphatically promised to complete an accreditation process on behalf of the institution, but each had failed to do so. The school community was broken, distrusting, suspicious, and hurting.

Another difficulty at the time of my arrival was that the school was sorely lacking in organizational infrastructure. One example was the student/parent policy that had been copied and pasted from other venues without edits—and certainly without consideration for whether they fit the school's context. Other examples include no school board policy manual, original bylaws did not resemble current functioning. There were no financial accounting policies and minimal compliance practices were being followed. Teachers and staff were afraid to make decisions—accustomed to a form of leadership closer to dictatorship than benevolent monarchy. And with an earlier push to web-hosted applications had come the overzealous decision to join the 21st-century by perfunctorily disconnecting the server, which had resulted in the loss of most of the data predating 2013. This to name only a few of the deficits. Had there been some strong organizational infrastructure in the 15-year history of Parkview, its evidence had vanished by the time I arrived.

I'll add to the concerns already mentioned some additional serious financial issues (even beyond owing the IRS a substantial amount of money and a loan that was being called due). Either no budget detail had been tracked, or it had been lost with the disconnection of the server. Either way, no documentation existed at that time. And, of course, under the circumstances there was no year-over-year data to drive decisions about forward or long-term financial planning. The only relevant item available in print was a one-page photocopy of summary line items, titled simply "budget" but bearing no relationship to the bookkeeping categories. After a lengthy and painstaking process of studying transaction-level detail for the years leading up to August 2013, several concerns were uncovered, among them:

1. Tuition receipts did not cover operational program expenses.
2. Distinct forms of untracked tuition discounts numbered five (staff, missionaries, multiple children, pastors, and private deals with the administrator).
3. A sizable deficit had been accrued by borrowing across fiscal years.
4. Teacher and staff salaries were the results of private deals.
5. Wages in general were extremely low.
6. There was no salary schedule, and there had even been periods during which payroll had not been met.
7. Four years of uncollected tuition debt had not been dealt with.

Not a single area of organizational infrastructure had a solid foundation in policy, process, or procedure. Yet it was precisely at this juncture that the resources of God's design came into play, reflected in foundations of (1) high-quality, Christ-centered education in the teaching staff, *where the rubber meets the road in terms of content*; (2) application of spiritual principles to relationship, *where the rubber meets the road in terms of process*; and (3) the implementation of technology for school management, *upon which a workable infrastructure could be built.*

I firmly believe that the survival of Parkview over the years, in the context of all that I have already described, can be attributed to a single factor: the powerful presence of Christ in the classroom environment, manifested through teachers with an unwavering commitment to teaching Christ in both content and process. There were many frustrations among families, but at the end of the day parents stuck it out because their children were learning and growing academically and spiritually—not to mention feeling safe and loved.

It is important to note that Parkview did not own any hard assets or cash reserves. And the prospect that a generous donor might, as it were magically, sweep into view to save the day would have constituted futile thinking. This isn't to say this *couldn't* have happened, but it would have been outright irresponsible to expect it. Why, after all, would anyone have wanted to invest in a prospect that appeared, and from the perspective of all outward indicators was, organizationally unsustainable? The Parkview board had only this question to answer: Was it being obedient? If the answer was yes, it had a mandate to move forward. If no, the only viable option was to cut its losses and shut down the operation. (Parenthetically, I invite any reader who might feel moved to invest financially in Parkview at the present time—I can make a strong case for that!—to contact me.)

Despite the seeming hopelessness of the situation from a fiscal standpoint, there was ample demonstration of unyielding and unwavering *chazown parats*. While having to deny organizational form, the school could rightly boast of the power and presence of Christ. Hmmm. Form denying power, or power *defying* form? Which to choose? Parkview had everything needed to survive and thrive, both organizationally and spiritually, provided this was God's will. And so it was . . . and so it did.

I could go on with details to support the evidence of doom and gloom, but what would be the point? Parkview was poised on the precipice of a seemingly bottomless pit, and outside observers at the time suggested that the entities of human force (money and influence) had taken actions that were about to nudge it into the abyss. Poppycock! Here was a situation demonstrating God—divine power—using the weakest entity in the eyes of the world—Jesus Christ *alone*—to confound those who were wise in their own eyes. He was applying to the situation a more than ample measure of Christ's power, in a group of believing people, to willingly and knowingly step off the edge—while trusting God and surrendering to His will. Pause with me for a moment to let your meditations marinate in the fullness of Jesus Christ and of His power—working in hearts *first,* and then bringing His power to bear on circumstances of form, second.

> "Behold, I send you out as sheep in the midst of wolves; so be shrewd as serpents and innocent as doves." (Matthew 10:16, ESV)

Nothing that has happened at Parkview can be attributed to any one person or group of persons possessing any particular gift or set of gifts. Nor can any of it be ascribed to the fantastic stories sometimes heard of the incredible faith of certain individuals earning them a mind-blowingly visible miracle inaccessible to people of weaker faith. Everything in this story may instead be attributed to the obedience of simple, child-like faith residing in people because God had given it to them of His own good pleasure, as a gift of His grace and not of works—just in case anyone might be tempted to boast (Ephesians 2:8–9).

There have been many exciting stories in the context of Parkview, some visibly miraculous and others not; in every case, though, they have been all about God working in spite of, not because of, people. As is typical, obedience to God has been evidenced not by exhilarating stories of favorable outcomes but by two consistent and dominating indicators in the lives of believers: steady, rigorous work addressing in each instance the next most important spiritual and structural challenges, one day at a time, without responding in fear of or attempted control over the unknown outcome; and ongoing, mutual admonishment, as necessary, to simply do that which is obedient (a rejection of fear and control), while trusting God and surrendering to His way and ends. That obedient and faithful way of life brings manna sufficient for the day and for the purposes of God's intended outcome. These indicators are (and have been) evident in the leaders at Parkview (teachers, board members, staff, and spiritually aligned families).

Christ's presence and power are very near when the "innocence of doves" characterizes operational functionality in decision-making and the "wisdom of serpents," rather than the outward appearance of circumstances, guides the discernment of underlying activators. This is particularly clear, as a reflection of Christ, during and after a season of vulnerability—a season "among wolves."

Please allow me to repeat: This kind of success is based not upon any merit in the people themselves but *only* on the merit of Christ and His power working in and through people. Therein lies the excellence of Parkview—though the school also offers a high-quality, Christ-centered education by teachers of *kata huperbole hodos* (the way beyond measure). No higher praise can be conferred upon a teacher—or on any human being—than that of their following that "most excellent way" (1 Corinthians 12:31).

I've chosen to end this book with a short summary of the wonderful works of God, in Christ, through the obedience of the believers of Parkview. Between August 2013 and April 2016 many events have transpired, of which I will mention only a few. I pray that this sampling will be sufficient to extol the power and presence of Christ in and through obedience.

In September 2013 the enrollment was 208—and by September 2015 it had risen to 325. Keep in mind that enrollment was 8 in 1997. As of April 15, 2016, the re-enrollment, plus the new enrollment, had exceeded that number. As I write, the leadership is scrambling to keep up with the facility demands created by the growth of the last two years, to continue to develop organizational infrastructure, and to address the burgeoning "to do" list for the coming year. Of necessity the board is considering the purchase of a building as a long-term upper school facility. The building is to be purchased (financed by the owner) in conjunction with the school still owning no hard assets or reserves. Allow me to mention, by way of icing on the cake, that the building itself is ideally suited to the strategic purposes of the school, without the astronomical costs of retrofitting. If that had not been ample enough evidence of a shower of blessings, this past week brought the offer of donated land for the purpose of athletic fields.

One might construe some of the decisions the board is making now—perhaps even going back to those of 2013—as irresponsible. But the narrow channel into which God drives His people as a result of obedience leaves them only two choices: to move forward or to capitulate by shutting down. (I'll mention at this point, incidentally, that the right choice in certain circumstances may actually be to pull the plug on an enterprise.) Only believing trustees are equipped to approach this decision—and then only after removing their shoes and falling to their knees in acknowledgment that the ground is holy.

Parkview has traveled an incredible distance since August 2013. The organization still has a long way to go, but the infrastructure is starting to take stable shape, the culture is healthy and thriving, a strategic plan is in place, the education continues to be of high quality, need-based tuition assistance is being provided, the governance structure is highly functional, staff compensation has improved, curriculum mapping is well under way, and a ten-year financial plan is taking shape according to research-based indicators of stability. Parkview is now accredited, State recognized, and an approved member of the Illinois High School Association. Extracurricular opportunities continue to expand in academics, athletics, and the arts, as does the ability to provide for the needs of diverse learners in the classroom. Four graduating high school classes are behind us, with the fifth only weeks away—and the K–12 portion of the school has almost doubled in size. Shut it down? How? In light of the showers of blessing that resemble a torrential downpour that would be like trying to plug an open fire hose with a pinky finger.

If you were to visit Parkview and ask the people "*How* did God do this?" they wouldn't be able to adequately respond from a data or strategy standpoint—because nothing about the outward indicators makes sense in connection with the outcome. However, they undoubtedly could and would identity the underlying activator as the powerful presence of Jesus Christ, according to the will of God, working in and through undeserving recipients of His grace and truth. The bottom line is that obedience to the command results in the fruit of the promise—without exception in spiritual, and at times also in temporal blessings. The greatest blessing before eternity—a rare and precious gem—is a dominating way of being Christ-like, otherwise stated, as I have sought to contend throughout this book, as a *graciously unapologetic* way of being.

> "It is of the LORD's mercies that we are not consumed, because his compassions fail not. They are new every morning: great is thy faithfulness. The LORD is my portion, saith my soul; therefore will I hope in him." (Lamentations 3:22–24, KJV)

Just as my father told me in the sixth grade, it doesn't matter who attends the Christian school as long as the believers who run the school are faithful. So I challenge each reader—both organizationally and spiritually—to consider whether the school with which you are affiliated is faithful to Christ alone. This is to disavow all human ways by rejecting fear and choosing Christ's way in *agapao.* The result is to live in the powerful presence of Jesus Christ, nourished by the fullness of His grace and truth, as the "sweet aroma of Christ among those who are being saved and those who are perishing" (2 Corinthians 2:15) wafts upward to the throne of God.

Be graciously unapologetic: when it's inconvenient; when it's scary; when it threatens tradition; when it rubs against the group norm; when it isn't culturally relevant; when the school is in organizational crisis or in a season of stability; and even when the vision of Christ *alone* isn't, well, sexy enough to inspire the masses.

> "Only let your manner of life be worthy of the gospel of Christ, so that whether I come and see you or am absent, I may hear of you that you are standing firm in one spirit, with one mind striving side by side for the faith of the gospel, and not frightened in anything by your opponents. This is a clear sign to them of their destruction, but of your salvation, and that from God. For it has been granted to you that for the sake of Christ you should not only believe in him but also suffer for his sake, engaged in the same conflict that you saw I had and now hear that I still have." (Philippians 1:27–30, ESV)

The happening truth at Parkview is that the school has engaged in the same conflict that early believers saw and heard about in Paul. For the sake of Christ—believing in Him but also willing to suffer for His sake (by grace, through faith)—they stood in one spirit, striving for the faith of the gospel, and were not overcome with fear because of their opponents. How could that possibly be a negative story, even if it were not God's will that the school should survive and thrive? The evidence of faith (which is of God and not of human agency) in rejecting fear in the face of Christ's opponents is a clear sign of salvation. The lives of believers as Christian educators—or as engaged in any other legitimate application—showcases the inestimable worth of the gospel of Jesus Christ by its ability to make us bold in truth and silent in sacrifice—in short, to make us like Him!

I am aware that the Bible itself does not contain the familiar picture of the lion and the lamb lying down together, though it certainly paints this portrait in spirit (Isaiah depicts the scene of the wolf and the lamb, followed by a picture of the lion eating straw like the ox; see Isaiah 11:6–7; 65:25); sometimes I smile to myself, thinking it *should* be there. Because the Lamb of God and the Lion of Judah coexist perfectly and fully in Jesus Christ, and because He is working within believers to produce in them the spiritual strength to wield the truth and yield in grace, it really does begin to feel as though the two species are bedded down together in our hearts.

The sensitized conscience of a human being conceived and born in sin tends to hear an accusation in every wafting breeze, in the creak of every door, and in every wailing howl; to see it in every shadow, flashing light, and wicked act; and to feel it in every incidence of writhing pain, in every rapid heartbeat, and in the crushing weight of a cursed earth, whose axis spins infinitely beyond the confines of human control. But within the believer reverberates the calming intonations of the Lamb, declaring, "There is therefore now no condemnation to those who are in Christ" (Romans 8:1), as well as the commanding voice of the Lion, proclaiming, "I have prevailed to open the scrolls and its seven seals" (Revelations 5:5).

What if believing educators were to refuse to entertain the human voice of fear, to instead listen intently to the voice of Christ, responding with *agapao* and resigning their lives to one long pursuit toward lion-hearted boldness against puffed up imaginations, along with lamb-like silence in the face of any abuses that might result? What if they were to pursue *only* that, applied to all their work in Christian education or to whatever else they may endeavor? This kind of witness, multiplied exponentially in a resounding chorus of voices from God's faithful people, might conceivably change the world (again) or even speed the day of Christ's return. Whichever is God's will, may He take us captive to the obedience of Christ and radically free us from our fears, so that we may as His people grow steadily toward the boldness of the Lion and the quietness of the Lamb.

> "Pray then like this: 'Our Father in heaven, hallowed by your name. Your kingdom come, your will be done, on earth as it is in heaven.'" (Matthew 6:9–10, ESV)

ACKNOWLEDGMENT

A more Biblically consistent Christian school model has been on my mind for a very long time. Looking back, I see the hand of God moving me in that direction with fierce intensity. I thank God for all the purifying fires that have resulted in this deeply satisfying work in Christian education.

The thoughts of this book can be traced to their earliest roots in my father, Rev. John J. Byker, 1924–2010, and my mother, Dorothy Joan Byker (Ronda), 1928–present. Thank you, Mom and Dad. Like so many of your time, you spoke easily of Reformation. But I extend you my gratitude primarily because you were continuously open to re-formation, within the blessed context of resting in Christ *alone*.

The *way of being* described in this book was most poignantly developed while acting functionally as a parent to several children in the aftermath of personal traumas. Thank you Joel, Jessica, and Christian Benson; Carmen and Christa Byker; Joey Vanden Bos; and Herwine Lamelus for having the courage to reject your fears and receive love in grace and truth. Your adult lives reflect the astounding redemptive power of Christ in unique ways and against all odds. Until eternity I will have no greater privilege than loving you and yours, in grace and truth.

Thank you to Mary (Byker) Arnhart and Larry Arnhart for the countless days and ways in which you have sheltered me and mine. From your lives I have learned much of what I know today about a Christ-like way. My life was a disaster, and I found in you God's astounding provision through your selfless hearts.

Last but certainly not least, I appreciate both of you deeply, Chad and Heather Dirkse. Thanks for the countless hours of dialogue, for embracing the pain of loving me, and for your firm grip on grace and truth, selflessly shared. When I think of "graciously unapologetic," both your faces materialize in my mind's eye. And thanks, Chad, for the title of the book!

ENDNOTES

Chapter 1

1 Isaiah 40:31 "Yet those who wait for the Lord Will gain new strength; They will mount up with wings like eagles, They will run and not get tired, They will walk and not become weary." (NASB)

2 Psalm 78:4 "We will not hide them from their children, but tell to the coming generation the glorious deeds of the Lord, and his might, and the wonders that he has done." (ESV)

3 Proverbs 4:23 "Above all else, guard your heart, for everything you do flows from it." (NIV)

4 Ephesians 2:8 "For you are saved by grace through faith, and this is not from yourselves; it is God's gift." (HCSB)

5 Proverbs 3:5–6 "Trust in the Lord with all your heart, and do not lean on your own understanding. In all your ways acknowledge him, and he will make straight your paths." (ESV)

Matthew 23:23–24 "'Woe to you, scribes and Pharisees, hypocrites! You pay a tenth of mint, dill, and cumin, yet you have neglected the more important matters of the law—justice, mercy, and faith. These things should have been done without neglecting the others.'" (HCSB)

6 John 1:14 "And the Word became flesh, and dwelt among us, and we saw His glory, glory as of the only begotten from the Father, full of grace and truth." (NASB)

7 2 Corinthians 12:9 "But He said to me, 'My grace is sufficient for you, for power is perfected in weakness.' Therefore, I will most gladly boast all the more about my weaknesses, so that Christ's power may reside in me." (HCSB)

8 Philippians 3:9 ". . . and be found in Him, not having a righteousness of my own from the law, but one that is through faith in Christ—the righteousness from God based on faith." (HCSB)

9 Matthew 22:37–39 "He said to him, 'love the Lord your God with all your heart, with all your soul, and with all your mind. This is the greatest and most important command. The second is like it: Love your neighbor as yourself.'" (HCSB)

Chapter 2

1 Matthew 22:36-40 "He said to him, 'Love the Lord your God with all your heart, with all your soul, and with all your mind. This is the greatest and most important command. The second is like it: Love your neighbor as yourself.'" (HCSB)

1 John 4:18 "There is not fear in love; instead, perfect love drives out fear, because fear involves punishment. So the one who fears has not reached perfection in love." (HCSB)

2 John 21:15–17 "So when they had dined, Jesus saith to Simon Peter, Simon, [son] of Jonas, lovest thou me more than these? He saith unto him, Yea, Lord; thou knowest that I love thee. He saith unto him, Feed my lambs. He saith to him again the second time, Simon, [son] of Jonas, lovest thou me? He saith unto him, Yea, Lord; thou knowest that I love thee. He saith unto him, Feed my sheep. He saith unto him the third time, Simon, [son] of Jonas, lovest thou me? Peter was grieved because he said unto him the third time, Lovest thou me? And he said unto him, Lord, thou knowest all things; thou knowest that I love thee. Jesus saith unto him, Feed my sheep." (KJV)

3 Acts 2:44–47 "And all who believed were together and had all things in common. And they were selling their possessions and belongings and distributing the proceeds to all, as any had need. And day by day, attending the temple together and breaking bread in their homes, they received their food with glad and generous hearts, praising God and having favor with all the people. And the Lord added to their number day by day those who were being saved." (ESV)

4 Matthew 13:24–30 "He put another parable before them, saying, 'The kingdom of heaven may be compared to a man who sowed good seed in his field, but while his men were sleeping, his enemy came and sowed weeds among the wheat and went away. So when the plants came up and bore grain, then the weeds appeared also. And the servants of the master of the house came and said to him, "Master, did you not sow good seed in your field? How then does it have weeds?" He said to them, "An enemy has done this." So the servants said to him, "Then do you want us to go and gather them?" But he said, "No, lest in gathering the weeds you root up the wheat along with them. Let both grow together until the harvest, and at harvest time I will tell the reapers, Gather the weeds first and bind them in bundles to be burned, but gather the wheat into my barn."'" (ESV)

5 1 Samuel 16:7 "But the LORD said to Samuel, 'Do not look on his appearance or on the height of his stature, because I have rejected him. For the LORD sees not as man sees: man looks on the outward appearance, but the LORD looks on the heart.'" (ESV)

6 Romans 3:9–11 "What then? Are we Jews any better off? No, not at all. For we have already charged that all, both Jews and Greeks, are under sin, as it is written: 'None is righteous, no, not one; no one understands; no one seeks for God.

All have turned aside; together they have become worthless; no one does good, not even one.'" (ESV)

7 Ephesians 2:8–10 "For by grace you have been saved through faith. And this is not your own doing; it is the gift of God, not a result of works, so that no one may boast. For we are his workmanship, created in Christ Jesus for good works, which God prepared beforehand, that we should walk in them." (ESV)

8 John 17:17–19 "'Sanctify them in the truth; your word is truth. As you sent me into the world, so I have sent them into the world. And for their sake I consecrate myself, that they also may be sanctified in truth.'"

9 John 21:15–17 "When they had finished breakfast, Jesus said to Simon Peter, 'Simon, son of John, do you love me more than these?' He said to him, 'Yes, Lord; you know that I love you.' He said to him, 'Feed my lambs.' He said to him a second time, 'Simon, son of John, do you love me?' He said to him, 'Yes, Lord; you know that I love you.' He said to him, 'Tend my sheep.' He said to him the third time, 'Simon, son of John, do you love me?' Peter was grieved because he said to him the third time, 'Do you love me?' and he said to him, 'Lord, you know everything; you know that I love you.' Jesus said to him, 'Feed my sheep.'" (ESV)

10 Colossians 1:16–17 "For by Him all things were created, *both* in the heavens and on earth, visible and invisible, whether thrones or dominions or rulers or authorities—all things have been created through Him and for Him. He is before all things, and in Him all things hold together." (NASB)

11 Matthew 23:23–24 "'Woe to you, scribes and Pharisees, hypocrites! For you tithe mint and dill and cummin, and have neglected the weightier provisions of the law: justice and mercy and faithfulness; but these are the things you should have done without neglecting the others. You blind guides, who strain out a gnat and swallow a camel!'" (NASB)

Chapter 3

1 Romans 9:6–8 "But *it is* not as though the word of God has failed. For they are not all Israel who are *descended* from Israel; nor are they all children because they are Abraham's descendants, but: "THROUGH ISAAC YOUR DESCENDANTS WILL BE NAMED." That is, it is not the children of the flesh who are children of God, but the children of the promise are regarded as descendants." (NASB)

2 John 3:3 "Jesus answered and said to him, 'Truly, truly, I say to you, unless one is born again he cannot see the kingdom of God.'" (NASB)

3 2 Corinthians 5:17 "Therefore, if anyone *is* in Christ, *he is* a new creation; old things have passed away; behold, all things have become new." (NKJV)

4 Exodus 20:10 ". . . but the seventh day is a Sabbath to the LORD your God. On it you shall not do any work, you, or your son, or your daughter, your male servant, or your female servant, or your livestock, or the sojourner who is within your gates." (ESV)

5 1 Chronicles 22:2 "David commanded to gather together the resident aliens who were in the land of Israel, and he set stonecutters to prepare dressed stones for building the house of God." (ESV)

6 2 Chronicles 2:17–18 " Then Solomon counted all the resident aliens who were in the land of Israel, after the census of them that David his father had taken, and there were found 153,600. Seventy thousand of them he assigned to bear burdens, 80,000 to quarry in the hill country, and 3,600 as overseers to make the people work." (ESV)

7 Acts 3:11 "Now as the lame man who was healed held on to Peter and John, all the people ran together to them in the porch which is called Solomon's, greatly amazed." (NKJV)

Acts 5:12 "And through the hands of the apostles many signs and wonders were done among the people. And they were all with one accord in Solomon's Porch." (NKJV)

Chapter 4

1 Deuteronomy 23:7–8 "You shall not abhor an Edomite, for he is your brother. You shall not abhor an Egyptian, because you were a sojourner in his land. Children born to them in the third generation may enter the assembly of the LORD." (ESV)

2 Joshua 8:30–35 "At that time Joshua built an altar to the LORD, the God of Israel, on Mount Ebal, just as Moses the servant of the LORD had commanded the people of Israel, as it is written in the Book of the Law of Moses, 'an altar of uncut stones, upon which no man has wielded an iron tool.' And they offered on it burnt offerings to the LORD and sacrificed peace offerings. And there, in the presence of the people of Israel, he wrote on the stones a copy of the law of Moses, which he had written. And all Israel, sojourner as well as native born, with their elders and officers and their judges, stood on opposite sides of the ark before the Levitical priests who carried the ark of the covenant of the LORD, half of them in front of Mount Gerizim and half of them in front of Mount Ebal, just as Moses the servant of the LORD had commanded at the first, to bless the people of Israel. And afterward he read all the words of the law, the blessing and the curse, according to all that is written in the Book of the Law. There was not a word of all that Moses commanded that Joshua did not read before all the assembly of Israel, and the women, and the little ones, and the sojourners who lived." (ESV)

3 Numbers 15:14–15 "And if a stranger is sojourning with you, or anyone is living permanently among you, and he wishes to offer a food offering, with a pleasing aroma to the LORD, he shall do as you do. For the assembly, there shall be one statute for you and for the stranger who sojourns with you, a statute forever throughout your generations. You and the sojourner shall be alike before the LORD." (ESV)

4 Ezekiel 47:21–23 "So you shall divide this land among you according to the tribes of Israel. You shall allot it as an inheritance for yourselves and for the sojourners who reside among you and have had children among you. They shall be to you as native-born children of Israel. With you they shall be allotted an inheritance among the tribes of Israel. In whatever tribe the sojourner resides, there you shall assign him his inheritance, declares the Lord God." (ESV)

5 Exodus 12:49 "There shall be one law for the native and for the stranger who sojourns among you." (ESV)

6 Psalm 94:6 "They kill the widow and the sojourner, and murder the fatherless." (ESV)

7 Deuteronomy 24:19–22 "When you reap your harvest in your field and forget a sheaf in the field, you shall not go back to get it. It shall be for the sojourner, the fatherless, and the widow, that the Lord your God may bless you in all the work of your hands. When you beat your olive trees, you shall not go over them again. It shall be for the sojourner, the fatherless, and the widow. When you gather the grapes of your vineyard, you shall not strip it afterward. It shall be for the sojourner, the fatherless, and the widow. You shall remember that you were a slave in the land of Egypt; therefore I command you to do this." (ESV)

8 Jeremiah 22:3 "Thus says the Lord, 'Do justice and righteousness, and deliver the one who has been robbed from the power of *his* oppressor. Also do not mistreat *or* do violence to the stranger, the orphan, or the widow; and do not shed innocent blood in this place.'" (NASB)

9 Malachi 3:5 "'Then I will draw near to you for judgment. I will be a swift witness against the sorcerers, against the adulterers, against those who swear falsely, against those who oppress the hired worker in his wages, the widow and the fatherless, against those who thrust aside the sojourner, and do not fear me, says the Lord of hosts.'" (ESV)

10 Deuteronomy 1:16 "Then I charged your judges at that time, saying, 'Hear the cases between your fellow countrymen, and judge righteously between a man and his fellow countryman, or the alien who is with him.'" (NASB)

11 Deuteronomy 24:14–15 "You shall not oppress a hired worker who is poor and needy, whether he is one of your brothers or one of the sojourners who are in your land within your towns. You shall give him his wages on the same day, before the sun sets (for he is poor and counts on it), lest he cry against you to the Lord, and you be guilty of sin." (ESV)

Chapter 5

1 John 1:5 "And the light shines in the darkness, and the darkness did not comprehend it." (KJV)

2 Hebrews 4:12 "For the word of God is living and active, sharper than any two-edged sword, piercing to the division of soul and of spirit, of joints and of marrow, and discerning the thoughts and intentions of the heart." (ESV)

3 John 1:12–13 "But as many as received him, to them gave he power to become the sons of God, [even] to them that believe on his name: Which were born, nor of blood, nor of the will of the flesh, nor of the will of man, but of God." (KJV)
4 John 1:10 "He came unto his own, and his own received him not." (KJV)
5 1 John 2:19 "They went out from us, but they were not of us; for if they had been of us, they would have continued with us. But they went out, that it might become plain that they all are not of us." (ESV)
6 Matthew 22:11–14 "But when the king came in to look at the guests, he saw there a man who had no wedding garment. And he said to him, 'Friend, how did you get in here without a wedding garment?' And he was speechless. Then the king said to the attendants, 'Bind him hand and foot and cast him into the outer darkness. In that place there will be weeping and gnashing of teeth.' For many are called, but few are chosen." (ESV)

Chapter 6

1 Isaiah 53:3 "He was despised and rejected by mankind, a man of suffering, and familiar with pain. Like one from whom people hide their faces he was despised, and we held him in low esteem." (NIV)
2 Matthew 23:27 "'Woe to you, scribes and Pharisees, hypocrites! You are like whitewashed tombs, which appear beautiful on the outside, but inside are full of dead men's bones and every impurity.'" (HSBC)
3 Jeremiah 6:14 "They have treated My people's brokenness superficially, claiming, "Peace, peace," when there is no peace." (HSBC)
4 1 Peter 2:8 "and a stone to stumble over, and a rock to trip over. They stumble because they disobey the message; they were destined for this." (HSBC)
5 Luke 14:26–27 "'If anyone comes to Me and does not hate his own father and mother, wife and children, brothers and sisters—yes, and even his own life—he cannot be My disciple. Whoever does not bear his own cross and come after Me cannot be My disciple.'" (HSBC)
6 Isaiah 55:11 "so My word that comes from My mouth will not return to Me empty, but it will accomplish what I please and will prosper in what I send it to do." (HSBC)
7 John 18:35–37 "Pilate answered, 'Am I a Jew? Your own nation and the chief priests have delivered you over to me. What have you done?' Jesus answered, 'My kingdom is not of this world. If my kingdom were of this world, my servants would have been fighting, that I might not be delivered over to the Jews. But my kingdom is not from the world.' Then Pilate said to him, 'So you are a king?' Jesus answered, 'You say that I am a king. For this purpose I was born and for this purpose I have come into the world—to bear witness to the truth. Everyone who is of the truth listens to my voice.'" (ESV)

8 Romans 3:9–10 "What then? Are we Jews any better off? No, not at all. For we have already charged that all, both Jews and Greeks, are under sin, as it is written: 'None is righteous, no, not one.'" (ESV)
9 Ephesians 2:8–9 "For by grace you have been saved through faith. And this is not your own doing; it is the gift of God, not a result of works, so that no one may boast." (ESV)
10 John 17:17 "'Sanctify them in the truth; your word is truth.'" (ESV)
11 Ephesians 6:10 "Finally, be strong in the Lord and in the strength of his might." (ESV)
12 Matthew 7:1–4 "'Judge not, that you be not judged. For with the judgment you pronounce you will be judged, and with the measure you use it will be measured to you. Why do you see the speck that is in your brother's eye, but do not notice the log that is in your own eye? Or how can you say to your brother, "Let me take the speck out of your eye," when there is the log in your own eye?'" (ESV)
13 Philippians 3:9 "and be found in him, not having a righteousness of my own that comes from the law, but that which comes through faith in Christ, the righteousness from God that depends on faith." (ESV)
14 Matthew 22:36–40 "'Teacher, which is the great commandment in the Law?' And he said to him, 'You shall love the Lord your God with all your heart and with all your soul and with all your mind. This is the great and first commandment. And a second is like it: You shall love your neighbor as yourself. On these two commandments depend all the Law and the Prophets.'" (ESV)
15 Matthew 19:26 "But Jesus looked at them and said, 'With man this is impossible, but with God all things are possible.'" (ESV)

Chapter 7

1 Proverbs 9:10–12 "The fear of the Lord is the beginning of wisdom, and the knowledge of the Holy One is insight." (ESV)
2 Romans 8:1 "Therefore, no condemnation now exists for those in Christ Jesus." (HSBC)
3 John 8:31–32 "So Jesus was saying to those Jews who had believed Him, 'If you continue in My word, *then* you are truly disciples of Mine; and you will know the truth, and the truth will make you free.'" (NASB)
4 Matthew 19:24–26 "'Again I tell you, it is easier for a camel to go through the eye of a needle than for a rich person to enter the kingdom of God.' When the disciples heard this, they were greatly astonished, saying, 'Who then can be saved?' But Jesus looked at them and said, 'With man this is impossible, but with God all things are possible.'" (ESV)
5 2 Timothy 2:15 "Be diligent to present yourself approved to God as a workman who does not need to be ashamed, accurately handling the word of truth." (NASB)
6 John 13:13–17 "'You call Me Teacher and Lord; and you are right, for *so* I am. If I then, the Lord and the Teacher, washed your feet, you also ought to wash

one another's feet. For I gave you an example that you also should do as I did to you. Truly, truly, I say to you, a slave is not greater than his master, nor *is* one who is sent greater than the one who sent him. If you know these things, you are blessed if you do them.'" (NASB)

7 1 John 2:6 "Whoever claims to live in him must live as Jesus did." (NIV)

8 Proverbs 3:5–6 "Trust in the LORD with all your heart, and lean not on your own understanding; in all your ways acknowledge Him, and He shall direct your paths." (NKJV)

9 John 14:6 "Jesus said to him, 'I am the way, and the truth, and the life. No one comes to the Father except through me.'" (ESV)

10 Ephesians 2:8–9 "For by grace you have been saved through faith. And this is not your own doing; it is the gift of God, not a result of works, so that no one may boast." (ESV)

11 Ephesians 1:5–6 "He predestined us for adoption as sons through Jesus Christ, according to the purpose of his will, to the praise of his glorious grace, with which he has blessed us in the Beloved." (ESV)

12 Philippians 1:6 ". . . being confident of this very thing, that He who has begun a good work in you will complete *it* until the day of Jesus Christ." (NKJV)

13 1 Corinthians 15:53 "For this corruptible must put on incorruption, and this mortal *must* put on immortality." (NKJV)

14 1 John 4:10 "In this is love, not that we have loved God but that he loved us and sent his Son to be the propitiation for our sins." (ESV)

15 Philippians 3:9–11 ". . . and be found in him, not having a righteousness of my own that comes from the law, but that which comes through faith in Christ, the righteousness from God that depends on faith—that I may know him and the power of his resurrection, and may share his sufferings, becoming like him in his death, that by any means possible I may attain the resurrection from the dead." (ESV)

16 Isaiah 64:6a "All of us have become like one who is unclean, and all our righteous acts are like filthy rags." (NIV)

17 1 Peter 1:13–16 "Therefore, preparing your minds for action, and being sober-minded, set your hope fully on the grace that will be brought to you at the revelation of Jesus Christ. As obedient children, do not be conformed to the passions of your former ignorance, but as he who called you is holy, you also be holy in all your conduct, since it is written, "You shall be holy, for I am holy." (ESV)

18 Hebrews 10:7 "Then I said, 'Behold, I have come to do your will, O God, as it is written of me in the scroll of the book.'" (ESV)

19 www.historyguide.org/intellect/allegory.html

20 Mark 2:17 "On hearing this, Jesus said to them, 'It is not the healthy who need a doctor, but the sick. I have not come to call the righteous, but sinners.'" (NIV)

21 Matthew 7:15 "'Watch out for false prophets. They come to you in sheep's clothing, but inwardly they are ferocious wolves.'" (NIV)

Chapter 8

1 Psalm 91:1 "He who dwells in the shelter of the Most High will abide in the shadow of the Almighty." (ESV)

2 Psalm 25:14 "The secret of the LORD *is* with those who fear Him, And He will show them His covenant." (NKJV)

3 Romans 8:1 "There is therefore now no condemnation for those who are in Christ Jesus." (ESV)

4 Romans 8:35–39 "Who will separate us from the love of Christ? Will tribulation, or distress, or persecution, or famine, or nakedness, or peril, or sword? Just as it is written, 'For Your sake we are being put to death all day long; We were considered as sheep to be slaughtered.' But in all these things we overwhelmingly conquer through Him who loved us. For I am convinced that neither death, nor life, nor angels, nor principalities, nor things present, nor things to come, nor powers, nor height, nor depth, nor any other created thing, will be able to separate us from the love of God, which is in Christ Jesus our Lord." (NASB)

5 Colossians 3:9–10 "Do not lie to one another, seeing that you have put off the old self with its practices and have put on the new self, which is being renewed in knowledge after the image of its creator." (ESV)

6 Romans 7:18–24 "For I know that nothing good dwells in me, that is, in my flesh. For I have the desire to do what is right, but not the ability to carry it out. For I do not do the good I want, but the evil I do not want is what I keep on doing. Now if I do what I do not want, it is no longer I who do it, but sin that dwells within me. So I find it to be a law that when I want to do right, evil lies close at hand. For I delight in the law of God, in my inner being, but I see in my members another law waging war against the law of my mind and making me captive to the law of sin that dwells in my members. Wretched man that I am! Who will deliver me from this body of death?" (ESV)

7 Ephesians 4:13 ". . . till we all come to the unity of the faith and of the knowledge of the Son of God, to a perfect man, to the measure of the stature of the fullness of Christ." (NKJV)

8 John 8:44–45 "'You are of your father the devil, and your will is to do your father's desires. He was a murderer from the beginning, and does not stand in the truth, because there is no truth in him. When he lies, he speaks out of his own character, for he is a liar and the father of lies. But because I tell the truth, you do not believe me.'" (ESV)

9 Ecclesiastes 2:11 "Yet when I surveyed all that my hands had done and what I had toiled to achieve, everything was meaningless, a chasing after the wind; nothing was gained under the sun." (NIV)

10 1 Corinthians 3:19–21 "For the wisdom of this world is foolishness before God. For it is written, '*He is* the one who catches the wise in their craftiness'; and again, 'The Lord knows the reasonings of the wise, that they are useless.' So then let no one boast in men. For all things belong to you." (NASB)

11 1 Peter 2:7–8 "Therefore, to you who believe, *He is* precious; but to those who are disobedient,

'The stone which the builders rejected Has become the chief cornerstone,' and 'A stone of stumbling And a rock of offense.' They stumble, being disobedient to the word, to which they also were appointed." (NKJV)

12 Philippians 1:27–28 "Only let your manner of life be worthy of the gospel of Christ, so that whether I come and see you or am absent, I may hear of you that you are standing firm in one spirit, with one mind striving side by side for the faith of the gospel, and not frightened in anything by your opponents. This is a clear sign to them of their destruction, but of your salvation, and that from God." (ESV)

13 Genesis 3:8 "And they heard the sound of the Lord God walking in the garden in the cool of the day, and the man and his wife hid themselves from the presence of the Lord God among the trees of the garden." (ESV)

14 Genesis 3:12 "The man said, 'The woman whom you gave to be with me, she gave me fruit of the tree, and I ate.'" (ESV)

15 1 John 2:6 "Whoever claims to live in him must live as Jesus did." (NIV)

16 Ephesians 3:20 "Now to Him who is able to do far more abundantly beyond all that we ask or think, according to the power that works within us . . ." (NASB)

17 2 Corinthians 10:5 "*We are* destroying speculations and every lofty thing raised up against the knowledge of God, and *we are* taking every thought captive to the obedience of Christ." (NASB)

18 1 Timothy 1:15 "The saying is trustworthy and deserving of full acceptance, that Christ Jesus came into the world to save sinners, of whom I am the foremost." (ESV)

19 2 Corinthians 2:14 "But thanks be to God, who in Christ always leads us in triumphal procession, and through us spreads the fragrance of the knowledge of him everywhere." (ESV)

Chapter 9

1 1 John 3:2 "Beloved, we are God's children now, and what we will be has not yet appeared; but we know that when he appears we shall be like him, because we shall see him as he is." (ESV)

2 John 15:12 "'My command is this: Love each other as I have loved you.'" (NIV)

3 Romans 6:1–2 "What shall we say then? Are we to continue in sin that grace may abound? By no means! How can we who died to sin still live in it?" (ESV)

4 Matthew 7:5 "'You hypocrite, first take the log out of your own eye, and then you will see clearly to take the speck out of your brother's eye.'" (ESV)

5 Luke 11:33 "'No one, when he has lit a lamp, puts *it* in a secret place or under a basket, but on a lampstand, that those who come in may see the light.'" (NKJV)

6 Galatians 2:20 "I have been crucified with Christ. It is no longer I who live, but Christ who lives in me. And the life I now live in the flesh I live by faith in the Son of God, who loved me and gave himself for me." (ESV)
7 Galatians 5:24–25 "And those who belong to Christ Jesus have crucified the flesh with its passions and desires. If we live by the Spirit, let us also keep in step with the Spirit." (ESV)
8 John 3:30 "'He must increase, but I must decrease.'" (ESV)
9 Philippians 2:6–7 "[Jesus Christ], though he was in the form of God, did not count equality with God a thing to be grasped, but emptied himself, by taking the form of a servant, being born in the likeness of men." (ESV)
10 http://www.auburn.edu/allynbaconanthology/documents/EchoNarcissus.pdf
11 Amos 7:7–9 "This is what he showed me: The Lord was standing by a wall that had been built true to plumb, with a plumb line in his hand. And the LORD asked me, 'What do you see, Amos?' 'A plumb line,' I replied. Then the Lord said, 'Look, I am setting a plumb line among my people Israel; I will spare them no longer.' 'The high places of Isaac will be destroyed and the sanctuaries of Israel will be ruined; with my sword I will rise against the house of Jeroboam.'" (NIV)
12 2 Corinthians 12:9 "But he said to me, 'My grace is sufficient for you, for my power is made perfect in weakness.' Therefore I will boast all the more gladly of my weaknesses, so that the power of Christ may rest upon me." (ESV)
13 Philippians 2:6–8 "[Jesus Christ], though he was in the form of God, did not count equality with God a thing to be grasped, but emptied himself, by taking the form of a servant, being born in the likeness of men." (ESV)
14 Psalm 34:8 "Oh, taste and see that the LORD is good! Blessed is the man who takes refuge in him!" (ESV)
15 Matthew 3:11–12 "'I baptize you with water for repentance, but he who is coming after me is mightier than I, whose sandals I am not worthy to carry. He will baptize you with the Holy Spirit and fire. His winnowing fork is in his hand, and he will clear his threshing floor and gather his wheat into the barn, but the chaff he will burn with unquenchable fire.'" (ESV)